The Epistle of

PAUL
THE APOSTLE

to the

PHILIPPIANS

GORDON KENWORTHY REED

The Epistle of Paul The Apostle to the Philippians

by Gordon Kenworthy Reed

©2022 Tanglewood Publishing

ISBN – 13: 978-1-7345087-9-6

TANGLEWOOD PUBLISHING

Fortressbk@aol.com

TANGLEWOOD
PUBLISHING

Book Design and Layout by Mieke Moller

Printed in the United States of America

CONTENTS

1

PERSEVERANCE
Philippians 1:1-11

As we begin to explore the book of Philippians, let me tell you a few things about the book, the author, and the occasion for its writing. Then I will also explain how we will approach this series.

As you know, this was a letter the great apostle Paul wrote to the church in Philippi, a city in Macedonia. The founding of that church is an exciting and interesting story as recorded in Acts 16. Paul and Silas came to Macedonia in response to a vision sent by God. Philippi was the first major city on the continent of Europe to receive the Gospel and have a Christian church planted there. Lydia, a prominent business woman from nearby Thyatira, was the first convert, and hers was the first household there to receive Christian baptism. Soon, a church began in her home and, amazingly, one of the first new members was the converted jailor who had imprisoned Paul and Silas by order of the city government. (Now don't get too excited about the fact that the only qualification the jailor had is that he beat up on the preacher before he became a member of the church.)

Many years later, Paul wrote this letter to that church while he was in prison awaiting trial before Nero. Philippians has often been called the epistle of joy. It is deeply and yet brightly theological in the best sense of the word. The truth of the Trinity is emphasized, the substitutionary atonement is presented, the supreme example of humility is demonstrated, and the core truths of the Christian life are illustrated through Paul's own ongoing experience of growing sanctification. The challenge to all believers to press on through discouragement, doubts, and fears is powerfully presented.

In the opening verses of chapter one, the Apostle offers prayers on behalf of the church and its members, expressing supreme confidence in God's great enabling power to take them through the trials of life all the way to heaven. This is the special focus of this chapter: God's persevering grace which enables us to persevere to the very end. Listen again to this promise from God's Word. "I thank my God upon every remembrance of you, always in every prayer of mine, making requests for you all with joy; for your fellowship in the Gospel from the first day until now, being confident of this very thing, that He who has begun a good work in you will complete it until the day of Jesus Christ."

Now let me offer you a beautiful and concise commentary on this passage from the Westminster Confession of faith.

"Those whom God has accepted in his Son and has effectually called and sanctified by his Spirit can never completely or finally fall out of the state of grace. Rather, they shall definitely continue

in that state to the end and are eternally saved. This endurance
of the saints does not depend on their own free will, but on God's
unchangeable decree of election flowing from His voluntary love.
It also depends on the effectiveness of the merit and intercession
of Jesus Christ, on the indwelling Spirit, and the indwelling seed
of God in the saints, and on the nature of the covenant of grace. All
these establish the certainty and infallibility of their preservation.
Nevertheless, the temptations of Satan, the world, and their
old carnal nature, along with neglect of the means of their
preservation, may lead believers to commit serious sins, and to
continue in them for a time. They consequently displease God and
grieve His Holy Spirit, have some of the fruits of God's grace and
His comforts taken away from them, have their hearts hardened,
and their consciences wounded, hurt and offend others, and bring
temporal judgments on themselves."

"I am confident of this very thing, that He who has begun a good work
in you will complete it unto the day of Jesus Christ." Is that really
true? How may we know?

I. PERSEVERANCE DEFINED

When we say that the Bible teaches that all true believers will
persevere to the end and surely be saved, just what do we mean? This
is the natural outgrowth from the doctrine of salvation as taught in
the Bible and is a part of salvation. It is linked with election, effectual
calling, regeneration, repentance, saving faith, justification, and
sanctification. In short, it is another piece of the whole, another part
of God's grand design. This means that all true believers, chosen in
Christ before the foundation of the world, regenerated by the Holy
Spirit, and united to Christ both in His death and resurrection, can

never fully or finally fall away from grace and salvation, but will most certainly persevere and be saved eternally in the end.

This does not mean that once you are a Christian you will never sin, nor does it mean you will always be in close fellowship with the Lord and walking in His will. We know both from Scripture and bitter personal experience that believers can and do sin and fall out of fellowship with the Lord. Moreover, when believers neglect prayer and the Word, when they neglect worship and grow lax in their service, they may and will fall into grievous sins and bring dishonor upon the Lord and His people, and even invite temporal and severe judgment on themselves, including sickness and even physical death. This falling away from fellowship may even endure for long seasons.

Nevertheless, if God has truly worked saving faith in your heart, and as such you are His child, then in the long run, nothing will be able to separate you from the love of God which is in Jesus Christ our Lord.

God will not allow you to remain forever out of fellowship with Himself. He may have to chastise you severely to bring you back to Him. It has been my experience that God has an unending supply of two-by-fours, and a fatherly will to use them when and where they will do the most good. Yes indeed, you may suffer much because of your sins and cause others to suffer as well, but sooner or later by gentle persuasion or with brickbats, like the prodigal of old you will awaken in your pig pen of sin, come to your senses, and return to the Father in deep, heartfelt repentance. If you are in the midst of deep conviction and wonder if God will ever forgive or take you back again, just remember His promise: "If you, then, being evil, know how to give good gifts to your children, how much more will your Father in heaven give good gifts to those who ask Him." God's good gifts to His children

include forgiveness, love, acceptance, and a glorious destiny. The same
Lord who commanded Peter to forgive his brother who sinned against
him seven times seventy will not require of us more than He will
supply to us. By the way, if you are deeply concerned about your sin
and grieved by your weaknesses, this is one token that you are indeed
a child of God.

All this sounds wonderful but what are …

II. THE GROUNDS FOR PERSEVERANCE

Just as our salvation is not based on our ability or our goodness, but
the free unmerited grace of God, so the foundation for our confidence
in the grace of perseverance is the shed blood of our Lord Jesus Christ.
His sacrifice was of such worth and power that it prevails for a full
and complete salvation. "I give them eternal life and they shall never
perish, neither shall any man pluck them out of my hand. My Father
who gave them to me is greater than all."

The certainty that the Lord will persevere in His good work of
salvation in us is also grounded upon his never-ceasing intercession
on our behalf. The greatest operative power in your life right now is
the prayer of the Lord Jesus on your behalf. Jesus said to Peter a few
hours before Peter's fall in denying Christ, "Simon, Simon, Satan has
desired you that he may sift you as wheat, but I have prayed for you…"
That was why Peter was restored after his grievous sin, and that's why
I have been restored, and why you have been and will be.

Our perseverance is also rooted and grounded in the character of God
Himself. "The Lord is faithful." These may be the greatest words in all
of the Bible. Then there is that beautiful benediction: "Now unto Him

who is able to keep you from falling and to present you faultless before the throne of His glory with exceeding joy." And, of course, these words from Philippians: "He who has begun a good work in you will carry it to completion until the day of Jesus Christ."

Finally, if you are predestined to be conformed to the image of Christ, who or what can separate you from the love of God which is in Christ Jesus our Lord? But doesn't this encourage people to live any way they want to live? The answer to that is simply this: Not if they have been born again by the Holy Spirit. Only a false confessor would use such a doctrine to presume on God's holiness and His love. The true believer when convicted of sin is miserable until that sin is confessed and true repentance begins to work itself out by God's Spirit.

III. HOW ARE WE TO USE AND APPLY THIS PRECIOUS TRUTH IN OUR LIVES?

The person who uses this doctrine as an excuse to sin is giving evidence of an unconverted heart. No, this blessed truth is not an excuse for indolence or willful sinning, but as an encouragement to godly living. Only assurance of this truth can enable you to live in peace and to live victoriously. If a wife is unsure of her husband's abiding love and care for her, that wife will live in fear and misery and be driven to despair. But if a wife is confident of love, feels accepted, knows her mistakes are forgiven, and knows that her husband's love for her is unshakeable, then she may live in peace and with joy. Her love for her husband and her desire to please him will be strengthened by her security in His love. Christ is that perfect bridegroom. We, the Church, are His bride. He is also the one true "friend who sticks closer than a brother." It is only the person who is secure in Christ's love that really grieves over sin and wants to quickly repent and return when he strays. It is only the certainty of forgiveness and love that brings us back into His presence to find relief.

Because you know that God will persevere in you and enable you to persevere in Him, not only is your salvation safe, but your life becomes increasingly filled with a desire to serve and honor Him, and your love grows ever deeper and stronger.

Questions for Discussion and Reflection

1. Discuss the meaning of perseverance in one's faith.

2. What is the basis for our confidence in the grace of perseverance?

3. What is the basis for our salvation?

4. This chapter discusses the fact that we sometimes fall out of fellowship with Christ. Discuss the ways in which God draws us back to Himself. What are some of the "good gifts" that he extends to His children?

5. If a person has been chosen as a child of God and rests in the assurance that he cannot be separated from Him, even after falling out of fellowship, what prevents that person from taking advantage of this assurance and living contrary to the way of God?

2

HOW TO PRAY
FOR YOUR CHURCH
Philippians 1:1-11

I have a fairly long list of churches Miriam and I pray for every day. Some of these churches are congregations I have pastored or supplied in the past. For the past several years, I have been supplying churches that are without pastors. There are many congregations where I have held mission conferences or Bible conferences, or have asked to do so in this coming year. There are other congregations whose pastors or elders have contacted me about various problems they are experiencing and have asked for prayer and counsel. But at the top of my list is the dear congregation of God's people in whose midst I have been called to serve at a given time. Miriam and I are both convinced that prayers of intercession for that specific body of believers and for each individual by name and by need (if we know of it) is the most important ministry we have on the congregation's behalf.

Every time I am away for any reason, my thoughts and prayers are always with that home congregation. When I hear of trouble in a church, I always ask, how am I to pray for that hurting congregation? How do I pray for those back home? These questions lead to another: How are Christians to pray for their church?

I often turn to the book of Ephesians for guidance, but thought it well to discover again how the apostle Paul prayed for the Church at Philippi as a guide for how we should be praying for our own churches. One thing is overwhelmingly clear to me and more so all the time: the most important ministry for all believers is to pray earnestly and without ceasing for their church. I sense we need to have special times for prayer together for God's guidance, and especially for constant filling of the Holy Spirit that we might fulfill our calling as a church.

I turn to a prayer of long ago which helps me to know how best to pray for congregations. In fact, it is a model prayer for all believers who love their church and want to see God's blessing on it. This prayer was first prayed by Paul for the Philippian church, and it is a classic of beauty and spiritual potential. In going over this prayer, I think how wonderful it will be when God sees fit to fulfill these things in all churches.

I. FIRST IS A PRAYER OF JOYFUL, LOVING THANKSGVING (vv. 3-8)

"I thank my God upon every remembrance of you." Memory is one of God's most precious gifts. It is a treasure house of rare jewels. It is the only garden that yields roses in the deepest winter cold. When we are careful to sow good seed in our lives, especially our relationships to each other, then we can enjoy a lifetime of beauty and thanksgiving.

So blessed had been their oneness in the Lord that the Apostle prayed for them with joy every time he prayed. Why? For many good reasons.

1. Because they were united with him in the furtherance of the Gospel. They shared his vision of a city and a world brought to Christ. Not only had these believers supported Paul when he was their pastor, but their love and prayers went with him even into his present prison cell. Indeed, they would follow him with loving tears as he took his last long walk on the Appian Way outside Rome. Do you realize how utterly powerless the preacher is without the prayers of his people? Do you realize the burden you bear when you hear the Word and do not obey it? The furtherance of the Gospel requires both sincere intercession for the messenger and, at the same time, eager willingness to obey the Word preached.

2. He was grateful because he knew that God would complete the good work of salvation in them, bringing them into glory with Him. They shared the same hope, the same confidence that one day they would meet in heaven.

3. In Tennessee years ago, two old men were saying goodbye for the last time, as one was nearing his death. Taking his friend by the hand, the dying old man said, "Lee, we have hunted these hills and fished these creeks together since we were just little boys, and we have been in Sunday school and church together all our lives. Goodbye old friend. We'll meet in heaven." And so they no doubt did.

So, the pastor and the congregation had shared their joys and sorrows, and most of all they shared the same grace that saves. Is there a closer tie in all the world than this? No wonder he would add, "I long for you all with the love of Christ."

II. IT WAS A PRAYER OF EAGER PETITIONS FOR THEIR BLESSINGS (vv. 9-11)

Here is where we learn to pray for our own churches. This is the heart of how to pray for each other, and to pray in confidence that God will indeed grant these requests.

1. "That your love may abound more and more in knowledge and discernment." Notice the careful wording of this request. He is not praying for an unthinking, blind love that tolerates all things and never attempts to distinguish between good and evil or right from wrong. The love for which he prays is intelligent, purposeful delight in God and His revealed will. And as that expresses itself in mutual love believers have for each other, it will include humility, tenderness,   compassion, and forgiveness in attitude; encouragement, truthfulness, and mildness in words; and self-denial, loyalty, and kindness in actions.

Notice also the word "abound." We are not to pray that little bits and pieces of these things may be found in a few people, but that this may be the obvious spiritual condition of the whole body and each member. And lest you try to exempt yourself from personal responsibility in these things, remember how one man, Achan, brought defeat and ruin upon all Israel because of his greed and sinful spirit.

My prayer is the "Achan" in all of us may be exposed, rooted out, and destroyed. And further, if you personally are the Achan in your congregation, that you may repent and deliver your soul before it is too late. As your ears hear these words, my prayer is that you will ask, "Lord, is it I?"

I know the Word warns us that knowledge without love puffs up the ego, but I also know that love without discernment can be frivolous and soon dissipated. So when we pray for each other, let's pray for that growing love between us and at the same time for knowledge of God's will and discernment in living it out.

2. "That you may approve (choose) the things which are excellent, and that you may be pure and blameless in the day of Christ." What in the world does this mean? It simply is a prayer that God's people may strive to be the best for God they can possibly be. Sadly, many Christians and many churches are satisfied to limp along from one year to the next, even from one generation to the next, without ever really counting for much in the progress of the Kingdom. A self-satisfied Christian is a worthless Christian, and a church that is content with the status quo is basically a dead church; certainly no threat to Satan, and no credit to the Lord. The Apostle adds "in the day of Christ" to remind us that we must all appear before the judgment seat of Christ to give an account of how we have lived our lives and how faithful to Christ's commands we have been as a congregation.

3. "Being filled with the fruits of righteousness which are by Jesus Christ, to the glory and praise of God." This final petition ends on a glorious and positive note. This is a prayer for a rich spiritual harvest in the Church and in each life. It is the fervent prayer of every farmer that he might have a reward for his hard work and vast investment, a really good harvest. It is my prayer as God's hired hand on His farm that you might reap an abundant harvest of love, joy, peace, long-suffering, kindness, goodness, faithfulness, gentleness, self-control, and the good works which flow out of these dispositions. We all need to pray that we will be a harvesting Church, seeking out the souls of people, bringing them to Christ and salvation. As we learn to abide

in Christ, we are promised that we will bring forth fruit, more fruit, and even much fruit. If the fruit is not there, neither is the abiding, but if the abiding in Christ is real, the fruit, the abundant harvest, will follow.

Why do we pray this way for one another? That one congregation may be glorified, admired, and spoken well of? God forbid! We pray this way that God may be admired, praised, and spoken well of. For after all, our whole purpose for being and for being a part of Christ's body the Church is that we may glorify God and enjoy Him forever.

Questions for Discussion and Reflection

1. Paul describes his relationship with the Philippians as a partnership. How does he define this partnership?

2. Why are knowledge and discernment critical to the growth of love among church members?

3. What are the characteristics of the kind of love for which Paul prays in verses 9-11?

4. Paul prays that the Philippians' love for one another may "abound." Why must this be "the obvious spiritual condition of the whole body and each member"?

5. Think back on the teaching in this chapter. What is the most important ministry for all believers? Why?

6. Do you have a ministry partnership with anyone in your life? If so, describe the partnership. Has it strengthened you in your ability to live a Gospel-centered life?

7. Consider your own church family. Would Paul rejoice in its partnership in the Gospel?

3

A HOLY TENSION
Philippians 1:12-30

The apostle Paul was in prison. One would hardly expect a man who was in jail for no fault of his own to be joyful. He was joyful. There is no other way to describe his attitude which shines through the words from Philippians. What an amazing man! Would any of us share his joy if we were in the same circumstances? His troubles were real and would be overwhelming to most of us. How could he express such exuberant joy and total confidence in the Lord's providence?

First of all, he did not give in to self-pity and allow himself to be defeated by his circumstances. He very easily could have given in to his troubles and allowed himself to be defeated by them. He could have been thinking about how unfairly he had been treated, and wondering why God had allowed him to suffer so much. After all, he was serving God and he was serving so well. He had traveled all over the Roman Empire, enduring unbelievable hardship and never-ending toil. Now he was in prison awaiting a trial before a mad man who hated Christ and all Christians. His prospects were very dim to say the least.

In the meanwhile, some professed believers were using Paul's troubles to advance their own cause and claiming glory for themselves where Paul had claimed none. Some were even mocking Paul and hoping the worst for him, but he did not allow any of these things to defeat him, nor did he engage in self-pity or complaint.

The next thing which gets our attention is that he looked upon all these negative things which happened to him as God's way of allowing him to serve Christ more effectively. Here he was in a prison cell, chained night and day to a Roman soldier. He had no relief night or day, nor any privacy at all. There are accounts of prisoners going utterly insane while enduring these things. But far from losing either his mind or his joy, he used this opportunity to bear witness to Christ, and did it so effectively that even some of Caesar's own household had come to faith in the Lord Jesus, and all the elite praetorium guard knew why Paul was in prison and heard the gospel from his own lips.

As for others who were preaching the gospel in Rome, he was pleased and thankful. He reasoned that even those whose motives were not pure were still preaching the gospel, so he was willing to trust the Lord and let Him be the judge. God's sovereignty was a reality for him and sustained him with confidence and joy. Let's look more closely at the man and his "world view."

I. PAUL'S OUTLOOK ON LIFE

His whole philosophy of life is summed up in these words: "For me to live is Christ." But what did that mean and how did it affect his mental and spiritual condition in such trying circumstances? Very simply, it meant that his purpose in life, his reason for living, was centered in the person of Jesus Christ and his relationship to his Lord. This meant his joy flowed from that relationship. His supreme interest was Christ. His hope was in Christ Jesus. He had found something far higher and nobler than his own self-centered interests and concerns. This gave him purpose, energy, and power. We all may speak of Christ being our all in all, but when that is really true, we are transformed and no longer conformed to this world and its values.

This was a very personal thing for Paul. It was not just a philosophical or theological statement; it was a personal commitment. Do you remember the stirring words of Joshua when he called Israel to commit whole heartedly to the Lord? "Choose ye this day who you will serve, but as for me and my house, we will serve the Lord." Now we hear Paul saying in like manner, "For me to live is Christ." When sincerely and consistently meant, these are words of power. Commitment to Christ must always be a deeply held personal decision that rises above all lesser causes and purposes. Does your life testify to that reality? Does mine? All of us have many goals and purposes, but this one must dominate over all others. To live for wealth, happiness, security, success, or whatever identifies us as people of this world who see nothing beyond the temporal and superficial. But to truly live for Christ and His kingdom will make lesser ambitions our servants, or rather His servants.   Remember, Paul worked for his living as a tent maker, but his purpose in life was not centered in career as such. Is this true of you?

Another way Paul expressed his life's purpose is found in these words which he wrote in this same letter: "That I may know Him and the power of His resurrection, and the fellowship of His suffering."

II. HIS VIEW OF DEATH

Death is a reality which we all must face. This man knew death was certain and probably even imminent. So we hear him say: "For me to live is Christ and to die is gain." Notice he did not say this in the same sense many have said similar words, such as, "Life is so horrible I wish I was dead." No, he was joyful. He hoped to live longer to serve Christ better. So there is nothing of weariness of life, even with all its trials and sufferings. Only the person who can sincerely say, "For me to live is Christ" may with equal sincerity say, "and to die is gain." For Paul, death would mean the fulfillment of all which he had sought in life. It would mean immediate and blessed fellowship with the Lord. It would mean higher, nobler service.

Never let Satan tempt you to think that life is so bad and so miserable that death would be preferable. It wasn't death Paul welcomed; it was anticipation of the conquest of death which Christ had won for him and the joy beyond. I say again, only the person who may truly say, "For me to live is Christ" may also add, "and to die is gain."

During one of the long drawn-out heat waves in Texas several years ago, people driving by a little country Baptist church in west Texas read these words on their sign board, "YOU THINK IT'S HOT HERE?"

Other words of Paul about death reveal exactly what he meant by these words, "to die is gain." He called death exchanging mortality for life. He said to depart and be with Christ is far better.

Later he would write: "I have fought a good fight, I have finished my course, I have kept the faith. Henceforth, there is laid up for me a crown of righteousness which the Lord, the righteous judge, shall give me at that day." The Lord shall preserve me unto His heavenly kingdom." Once more, I say only the person who can say, "To me to live is Christ" can expect better things after death.

In Shakespeare's well-known story of Hamlet, the hero is contemplating the fates of life, and musing with himself he begins his famous soliloquy with these words, "To be or not to be, that is the question." Don't think for a moment the Apostle was thinking the same thing as Hamlet. He was simply saying, since he had found out life was all about his relationship to the Lord Jesus, death held no fear for him. It's really too bad we think and say death is preferred over life only when life is so unbearable we can't stand it. For every believer, in every circumstance, at whatever age, the truth is "to die is gain"

III. THE HOLY TENSION

At this point, Paul begins to speak of his dilemma, this holy tension in which he finds himself. It is difficult for him to know which he prefers the most. To live and go on living will only mean more service to Christ and His Church. To die will be to pass into Christ's immediate presence and begin a far greater realm of service.

Ed Somerville survived fierce combat in the Pacific area during World War II. He came home, went back to college, married, and had a lovely wife and two precious little girls. During his senior year in seminary, he was diagnosed with terminal cancer. After graduation, he became assistant pastor at 1st Presbyterian Church in Macon, Georgia. He served there for a little over one year before he finally died. His father was a home mission pastor at a little mountain church near Weaverville, NC, where I grew up. Upon hearing of his son's death, his father, Walter Somerville, came by our church to tell Dr. Dendy of Ed's passing in these words: "Well, Henry, Ed's been promoted." And he had been. My own favorite verse of Scripture by far are these words from Revelation 22: "And His servants shall serve Him."

As death approaches, the Apostle sees himself as a boat ready to up anchor and set sail, or as a desert nomad, ready to strike his tent and move on to a fairer oasis. He longed to see Him face to face whom he has seen but darkly as through a glass. He knows that eye has not seen, nor ear heard, nor has it entered into the mind of man the things which God has prepared for those who love Him. Just to be with the Lord, that's enough.

However, with his customary modesty and humility, Paul also knows that for the Church, it would be better for him to remain for yet a while and continue to minister and serve. For unselfish reasons, it might be better to remain awhile and keep on encouraging the body of Christ. So, as usual, he lays aside personal preference and decides it would be better to do just this and postpone his own joy. God has heard his prayer and he is reassured he will remain, at least for a little while, that he might finish the work to which Christ called him.

So we are all caught up in this holy tension, aren't we? Not as Elijah who in deep depression called out to the Lord, "It is enough, now take away my life," but rather to testify by word and life, "For me to live is Christ and to die is gain."

Questions for Discussion and Reflection

1. What was the source of Paul's great joy, even as he was held in prison?

2. What did Paul mean by, "to die is to gain"?

3. Paul's life was fully and completely defined by the conviction, "for me to live is Christ." How was this philosophy reflected in the way he lived his life?

4. Is your life defined by this same conviction, or do worldly things have a greater influence? What are some concrete ways that you could bring Christ closer to the center of your life and daily living?

4

REJOICING IN ADVERSITY

Philippians 1:12-30

Someone has said, and I believe it is true, that the measure of spiritual maturity is revealed in our reaction to adversity. If this is true, the testimony of Paul in this particular part of Philippians 1 proves him to be perhaps the greatest Christian who ever lived. From the time Christ called him on the road to Damascus until the day he was martyred for the Faith, Paul's life was a long series of severe adversity in every imaginable way. Would you care to hear the short list of a few things he suffered?

"In stripes above measure, in prisons more frequently, in deaths often. From the Jews five times I received forty stripes, minus one. Three times I was beaten with rods, once I was stoned; three times I was shipwrecked; a night and a day I have been in the deep; in journeys often; in perils of water; in perils of robbers, in perils of my own countrymen; in perils of the Gentiles, in perils in the city; in perils in the wilderness; in perils in the sea; in perils among false brethren; in weariness and toils; in sleeplessness often; in hunger and thirst; in fastings often; in cold and nakedness; besides the other things that come upon me daily; my deep concern for all the churches. Who is weak and I am not weak? Who is made to stumble and I do not burn with indignation?"

Every time I read this, I burn with deep shame. What do I know of suffering for Jesus' sake, unless it is by "sleeplessness often, and the daily concern for the churches"? And this is the same man who wrote, "Rejoice in the Lord ALWAYS, and again I say, REJOICE." I think the most frequently witnessed reaction of Christians to adversity is not rejoicing but retaliation, and in this the Lord is never honored.

Paul begins this section by simply stating: "I want you to know, brethren, that the things which happened to me have actually turned out for the furtherance of the Gospel." Here there is no accounting of "the things which happened to me"; just that clipped sentence and then his reveling and marveling at how God had used his adversity for His glory and the spread of the Gospel.

I. THE EFFECT OF HIS BEING IN PRISON AND IN CHAINS

A. On the Roman Guards

Being in prison in ancient Rome was not a vacation, nor was it designed to preserve the dignity of the prisoner. For a man totally innocent of the trumped up charges brought against him by the corrupt Sanhedrin of the Jews, and of whom the civil rulers said, "This man has done nothing deserving of death or chains", Paul displayed a remarkable attitude toward his present condition of being in chains and on trial for his life. He did not linger over the very real miscarriage of justice, or the many humiliating treatments he had to endure. He displayed no bitterness or self-pity. You see, for this man, God's sovereignty in foreordaining all that comes to pass was not just a doctrine to proclaim and defend, but a life-shaping truth to live by.

He even sounded excited that "the whole praetorium guard" became aware that he was in chains because of his faith and his firm commitment to spreading the Gospel of salvation through Jesus Christ. The situation was something like this: The elite palace guard was selected from among the best of Roman soldiers. Their assignments included protecting the Caesar and guarding the important prisoners awaiting trial before him. The guards were chained to the prisoners four hours at a watch and they relieved each other on a regular basis, so that in a rather short time, every one of the guards would have been chained to Paul at least once and probably several times. You have to know that he would tell them his story and why he was in prison. I would guess that because of his demeanor of gentleness, courage, faith, and great joy they would have been deeply impressed and willing to listen to what he had to say. Even these veterans of many battles, hardened by their own suffering and the horrors they had faced in hand to hand combat, saw something special and unique in this man. What they were seeing and hearing was a man who had been transformed by the power of Christ and daily growing in likeness to Him. (Do people see this in you?) He was undoubtedly the topic of many conversations. The guards had family and friends and soon, as Dr. Hendriksen put it, "he and his cause became 'the talk of the town'."

B. The "Brothers in Christ"

These brothers were the believers living in Rome. The Church
had been in existence in Rome for several years. Earlier, Paul had
written to them what was to become the book of Romans, one of the
most important books in all the Bible. It is clear that many Gentiles
as well as Jews had been converted and congregations had been
established throughout the city. One can only imagine the difficulties
they faced trying to be faithful to Christ in such a place as Rome. By
implication, we gather the believers in Rome had become timid and
reluctant to speak out very much for Christ. At first, they distanced
themselves from Paul and not one of them stood by him at his first
hearing. Since the Gospel had become "the talk of the town," local
believers and preachers had become more bold to proclaim the Good
News, but from mixed motives.

But as is always the case, there were those who saw an opportunity
for self-aggrandizement. With Paul out of the way, this was their
chance to move to the forefront and take over the leadership in
the Church. Jealousy and contentions among Christians for places
of prominence and imagined importance is not a new story. This
same undercurrent was present among the twelve apostles and was
sternly rebuked by the Lord. It is evident from the book of Acts and
from many things Paul had said in some of his letters, that this was
a major problem throughout the whole realm of the Church. The
struggle for recognition and glory still goes on in the Church, and
especially among pastors and other leaders in the Church. This
is always to the harm, and even can be the destruction, of many a
promising ministry.

But, thank God, there were the pure in heart that saw the need for them to step up and stand in the gap. Paul said these were proclaiming Christ out of love and with goodwill while others were preaching with selfish ambitions, and even with the intent of "showing Paul a thing or two about who is really important." And Paul's reaction? He clearly recognized what was going on and said: "What then? Only that in every way, whether in pretense or truth, Christ is preached, and in this I rejoice, yes and will keep on rejoicing." Such an attitude and such a response only come from above, and from Christ dwelling richly in your heart by faith.

Paul's self-forgetfulness earns not only our admiration, but should inspire like behavior on our part. Indeed, it will if Christ is dwelling richly in our hearts, too. I wonder if we would hold this great man in such high esteem if he had responded to these self-centered brothers in like manner. He shows nothing of self-pity or self-justification because of the actions of these jealous preachers who were trying to build themselves up at his expense. Nor does he try to tear them down in the eyes of others. Rather, what really mattered to him was that Christ was being preached, and for this he rejoiced. Was he blind to what they were doing? No! Was he approving their ignoble ambition? No. He was simply focused on the Gospel so much that he could see the good that went beyond evil intent.

II. WHAT WAS HIS SECRET?

There really is no secret; just a few simple statements of faith and confidence found in verses 19-26. First of all, he had great confidence in the intercessory prayer of believers and the power of the Holy Spirit working through those prayers. He also knew that such prayers were being offered up continually on his behalf by the Church. Of course, he wanted to be free again to travel to the churches he had established and to regions beyond. It sounds as if he truly expected this to happen, but allowed for the fact he might be condemned. His highest ambition was that Christ would be glorified in his life, whether by life or death. That was obviously one of the foundation stones of his vibrant and joyful attitude. He put it this way: "For me to live is Christ and to die is gain." His whole life's purpose was to serve Christ in obedience to his heavenly calling. Until the day of his death, Paul always expressed amazement and wonder that the Lord had actually forgiven him for his terrible sins committed while persecuting the Church, and beyond that he would actually use Paul as His personal ambassador.

His one great longing in life was to at last reach heaven and enjoy the fellowship with the Lord Jesus. What can you do with a man who has no desire for personal fame and glory, and has no fear of death, but eagerly awaited his final union with Christ? Certainly persecution holds no fear for such a man. If he knows death is just God's way of bringing him home, how can you stop him?

That's why adversity could not defeat him, not even rob him of joy. In fact, so long as he suffered for Jesus' sake, he could and did rejoice in his sufferings. How about you and me? Can we rejoice in adversity, or do we merely endure it? That all depends on how sincerely you are able to say, "For me to live is Christ and to die is gain."

Questions for Discussion and Reflection

1. What fueled Paul's positive attitude in the face of imprisonment, and even because of imprisonment?

2. Paul's very manner of being, together with his ability to rejoice in the face of suffering, gave witness to his faith. Do you think others see the measure of your faith in your manner of being? Why or why not?

3. Why didn't Paul break under the strain of his suffering? What sustained him?

4. What does it mean to "conduct yourself in a manner worthy of the gospel of Christ?" (v. 27)

5

THE GIFT OF SUFFERING
Philippians 1:27-30

Have you ever thought of suffering as a gift from God? Probably not, but here in this passage, the apostle Paul said, "For to you it has been granted on behalf of Christ, not only to believe in Him, but also to suffer for His sake." And what really makes this so astounding is his choice of especially one word: "granted." Why? Because this word is almost always used in the Greek to designate a gift of superlative worth. But the gift of suffering for the Lord is preceded by the gift of faith in the Lord: "For by grace are you saved through faith, and that not of yourselves, it is a gift of God." So here in this verse, the same word is used to describe faith as a gift, and suffering as a gift.

Since Paul puts the gift of faith as first in order, so must we, for it is only for those who have received the gift of faith in Christ who may also receive the gift of suffering for Him, and understand that it is truly a gift to be treasured and for which to be thankful. Now, we would all agree that faith in Christ is indeed a precious gift, but to count suffering for Christ as a precious gift requires us to consider carefully what is being said, and to search our hearts before the Lord. The more I read the book of Acts and the various epistles of the New Testament, the more I am convinced that suffering for the Lord's sake is the norm and not the exception in the Christian life. Of course, I know that in God's kind providence we are spared much which many believers have endured, and continue to do so.

I. THE GIFT OF BELIEVING IN CHRIST

So what all is included in the "gift of believing" to which Paul alludes? Without going too far and wide and finding a text book definition of faith, we may simply look at the context of what has been said in this chapter of Philippians and get an insight into what Paul intends by this expression. Dr. Hendriksen in his incomparable commentary on Philippians describes "believing in Christ" in these words: "To rest on Christ, surrendering oneself to His loving heart, and depending on His accomplished work." He also adds the words, "genuine personal trust in the Anointed One."

The tense of the verb suggests both a once for all, and a continuing activity which never ceases, and isn't that how faith is? It is never static; it is ongoing, and "ongrowing," too. There was at least one man sitting in that Philippian congregation who would understand what Paul meant by these words when they were read on that Lord's Day long ago. He was an old man by this time, and the marks of strife and war could be seen on his body, for he had served the Empire as one of its soldiers. When his combat days ended, either by age or injury, he was made a prison guard in this same city. Then one day, word was sent that two dangerous prisoners were being committed to his charge and he must guard them well. When they were brought to him, beaten half to death, he seized them and had them chained and thrown into the depths of the dungeon. He would take no chances, for his own life would depend on keeping them safe for trial and execution the next day. He wasted neither time nor sympathy on these rascals, nor did it even cross his mind to ease their obvious suffering with water for their parched throats and oil for their lacerated backs.

Later that same night, a strange thing began to happen. Their barely conscious groans turned into songs, and not songs of sad lament as would be expected. The note of joy was all too obvious, and it grew stronger as they sang until the whole prison was filled with song and mirth. What mad men these! Who was this Jesus Christ to whom and of whom they were singing with such powerful joy? Then the earthquake struck and the foundations of the prison were shaken, the doors sprang open, and chains were loosened from their moorings, and the prisoners would surely escape at the cost of the jailor's life. He drew his sword, not to slay the escaping prisoners but himself, for he knew his life was forfeited. Then from the darkness within, a loud voice called out, "No, stop, do yourself no harm, for we are all here." Calling for a light, he ran in, fell down trembling before Paul and Silas, and brought them out and asked, "Sirs, what must I do to be saved?" He was told, "Believe in the Lord Jesus Christ, and you will be saved and your household." So he took them home and the rest of the night was spent in finding out what it meant to "believe in the Lord Jesus Christ." And before that night was over, he and all his had been baptized in the name of the Father, and of the Son, and of the Holy Ghost.

Truly, "to him it had been granted by grace to believe in the Lord Jesus Christ," and probably also by this time, "to suffer for His sake."

He had received that "gift of believing" long ago, and like the one who explained to him the way of salvation, "also to suffer for His sake," and how to react to that gift. So as that old but joyful saint heard those words read from his beloved pastor, I am quite sure a fervent amen was heard from his lips and tears of thanksgiving glistened in his eyes. So we, too, need to consider what form that gift of suffering may take and how we are to respond to its challenge.

II. THE GIFT OF SUFFERING FOR CHRIST'S SAKE

Suffering was the norm for believers of that era, and waves of deadly persecution swept back and forth over the little flock of Christ. Philippi would have been one of those places where these dark shadows fell, but not the only place. In fact, in every place where Christians lived, they were given the opportunity to suffer for Jesus' sake. Their stories are many and to read some of them is to weep. Stories of men and women being humiliated, tortured, and killed. Stories of once prominent men, revered and respected for their accomplishments, now despised, stripped of dignity and clothing and all earthly possessions and positions, dying under the sword and cross of Rome. Ah, yes, and stories of young women with babies at their breasts dying with their little ones for naming Jesus Christ as their Lord.

Suffering in itself is not a privilege or a gift, though it must often be borne, but suffering on behalf of Christ, for His sake and the Gospel's, is very different. Such suffering may well be not only a sacred duty, but also a gracious privilege for many reasons. First, it knits the heart of the sufferer even closer to Christ, and enables one to understand from the heart the One who suffered and died that sinners might live forever. All of us will suffer much in this life, but when the time comes to suffer for Jesus' sake, even in small ways, there is glory and deep joy.

Again, to suffer for Jesus' sake, even in the extreme, brings assurance of salvation and heavenly reward. Few have suffered more for Jesus' sake than John Hus of Prague on a July day in 1415. He had been assured of safe conduct by the authorities of Church and State if he would come and defend the doctrines of grace he had been preaching. But as soon as he entered the city, he was arrested, tortured, tried, and sentenced to burn at the stake. Even as Christ was reviled on his way to the cross and even after He had been lifted up to die, so John Hus was humiliated and chained to a stake. Before the fires were lit, the bishop placed a paper crown on his head with three faces of devils painted on it. Hus replied, "Did not my Lord Jesus bear a crown of thorns upon His head for my sake? Why should not I then bear this like a crown, ignominious though it be?" The bishop said, "I commit your soul to the devil." Hus answered, "But I," said Hus as he lifted his eyes towards heaven, "commit my soul into Thy hands, Lord Jesus." Then they covered him with pitch, and piled wood and straw around his body up to his neck before lighting the fire. He died with a litany of supplication on his lips.

Suffering also is a powerful testimony which has been used by the Lord to bring thousands into the Kingdom. Who could deny that Saul of Tarsus was deeply convicted by the brave death of Stephen, and so it has ever been down to this very day. Satan's delight in the death of believers for Jesus' sake is blighted by the way God uses such suffering for His own glory and the frustrations of Satan.

Now, what of us for whom the sort of suffering known by believers in Philippi and like places seems to be remote possibility? God's gift of suffering to you may be in much lesser ways and in smaller things, at least for now. Who knows how soon and fierce the deadly storms of cruel persecution may break over our heads? But it is ours for now to be faithful in the small but painful ways we are called upon to suffer for Jesus' sake. It is sad but true that most of the misunderstanding we experience, much of the reviling and mocking, will come from other Christians. That was happening to Paul. Even while in a Roman prison, other Christians were saying bad things about him, as they had from the moment of his conversion.

But the most likely form of suffering for Jesus' sake will be something like this. If you will simply take all your pain, sickness, weakness, disappointment, and grief and ask the Lord to use it, and dedicate to His service and glory, He will. Sing your songs of faith in the midnight hours of your life, and the prisoners will hear, and prisons of unbelief and hard stony hearts will be unlocked, and someone will ask you, "What must I do to have what you have?" You can surely tell them the answer. Then you will understand how precious the gift of suffering may be, and how powerfully God will use it for His glory and the "gathering of the elect," and the strengthening of weak believers.

Questions for Discussion and Reflection

1. What does it mean to suffer for Christ?

2. Why are we taught that suffering for Christ is a gift?

3. How might suffering for Christ look? (Hint: It does not have to be physical.)

4. Are there examples in your own life of suffering for Christ? Describe them.

5. How is believing in Christ a gift?

6

A MANDATE
AND A MODEL
Philippians 2:1-11

What a wonderful church it must have been in Philippi long ago.
It was founded by the apostle Paul and was most likely the first
congregation of believers in Jesus Christ on the continent of Europe.
Among its very first members was Lydia, whose heart God opened
to the Gospel, and the Philippian Jailor. There are references to
this congregation in other letters Paul wrote, and in these he speaks
in glowing terms of their generosity and faithfulness, and of their
loving concern for him and his needs. They had not only supplied
financial support, but had sent their love gift by sending one of their
own number, Epaphroditus, to Rome to inquire personally of Paul's
situation and to bring him reports from the Church. This good man
had made the long and often dangerous journey from Philippi to
Rome, and once in Rome had become seriously ill to the point it
seemed death was imminent. To Paul's great joy and to that of the
congregation in Philippi, God spared Epaphroditus. The point of all
this is to say that Paul was both very joyful to hear of the good things

he was told about the Church there, grateful for their loving gift but also somewhat concerned to hear of potentially serious problems which might hinder the witness of this important congregation.

The letter begins with joyful appreciation for the good things happening there, along with words of comfort and encouragement in face of opposition and persecution. There are also words of guidance and help which would serve to stave off possible troubles which might develop within the congregation. The Church there was both strong and fragile, which is always true of any congregation, including our own. It is strong because of our glorious head, the Lord Jesus and His promise to the Church. It is fragile because of Satan's unending attacks and our own weaknesses and sins.

In reading through this short letter, it is apparent that the Apostle was concerned for the Church because of the persecution to which they were subjected, the danger of false teachers creeping in, and the personal differences between members which might lead to division within the Church. What the lady Euodia and the lady Syntyche were arguing about we have no idea, yet we do get the idea they were both strong-willed ladies who seemed to be vying for control or position. And so the Apostle, later in this letter, will appeal to them to make peace for the Lord's sake and for His body's sake.

But are these not the very same dangers which may face any given congregation of God's people including our very own: persecution from without, false teaching and divisions from within? It is amazing to me how "current" the Bible is, and how it addresses situations which are common to all believers. In this passage, it appears that the Apostle was attempting to administer preventive medication before a dangerous infection of division could decimate the Church.

But rather than reprimanding them, as he was most certainly capable of doing and as believers in other congregations could bear witness, he encouraged and exhorted them in a positive way to seek those qualities which would produce harmony and Christ-likeness.

I. THE REMINDER OF PAST BLESSINGS

This reminder is couched in the language of reflection. It was as if the Apostle was saying, "First of all, I want you to stop and consider the personal blessings you have in Christ. Have you received from Christ any consolation and the comfort of His love in all your trials and tribulation? Have you known the fellowship of the Holy Spirit and that which is produced among believers by the indwelling Spirit? Have you had any experience of the tender mercy and compassion of Christ?" These are self-answering questions. Of course they had. So what's the point? Well, if you have received these gracious gifts from the Lord of mercy and grace, why are you hesitant to deal in like manner with your brothers and sisters in Christ? Doesn't God's gracious dealing with you put you in a position of debt to Him? Doesn't this teach you and motivate you in your dealings with fellow believers? Most certainly, each time go to the Lord's Table, we are reminded that we have received all these mercies from our dear Lord, and so are in debt to Him and to each other to behave as becomes followers of Christ.

II. THE APPEAL FOR NEEDED GRACES

Based on these realities of grace, the Apostle calls on us to manifest them in our relationship to each other within the body of Christ. The appeal is three-fold and always important in any congregation of God's people, and the more so when there is an absence of these graces, or even just a shortage of them. What a fitting appeal for us as we gather around the Lord's Table. The Apostle had been rejoicing in all that God had done and was doing in this beloved congregation, but now he made this request, "Make my joy full." This would gently suggest that as well as things were going in the Church, there were some tendencies which could cause problems, and may even then have been threatening the Body life. Isn't it amazing that it was not the prospect of being released from prison which would "make his joy full," but the prospect of seeing deep unity and beautiful harmony within the congregation Paul loved?

The first of these requests was for oneness or a deep unity within the body ... " Being like-minded, having the same love, being of one accord, of one mind." When there is an inner disposition towards each other with a desire for unity based on truth, then there will grow out of that like-mindedness a mutual love for Christ, and therefore for each other, which was the special emphasis here. This brings harmony of thought, emotion, and purpose, "being of one accord, of one mind." Truly, as the Psalm reads, "Behold how good and pleasant it is when brothers (and sisters) dwell together in unity."

This is impossible without lowliness of mind or humility on the part of all concerned, which is the second grace requested in this three-fold appeal. "Let nothing be done from selfish ambition or empty conceit." What a powerful and convicting phrase. Oh how much good could be done if no one cared who received the credit. Oh how easily we want to claim control and ownership of that which belongs to Christ and the whole body. I wish we all knew how vitally important this admonition is not only for the unity of the body but for its effectiveness in the world, and for the honor of Christ. I believe more is said concerning this humility than any other one virtue mentioned by Christ and His apostles, yet it is the least heeded by most of us.

The positive way of presenting this same virtue is stated this way, "But in lowliness of mind, let each esteem others better than himself." The temptation is always to respond, "But Lord, wouldn't that be hypocritical of me when I know I'm smarter, sweeter, more godly, and certainly more humble than anyone else in this Church?" (A young lady, who was very conscious of a beauty few others thought she possessed, told the photographer, "Now just do me justice in this portrait." To which the poor fellow responded, under his breath of course, "What you need is mercy not justice.")

The final needed grace which grows out of the other two is helpfulness to each other. Paul put it this way: "Let each of you look out not only for his own interests, but also for the interests of each other." How zealous are you to reach out to each other, even sacrificially striving to assist and minister to each other in every known need? Always be working to improve this and enlarge it, that no one is overlooked. Just stop and think how much the Lord Jesus loved that unlovable brother or sister. He died for that one!

III. THE EXAMPLE OF JESIS CHRIST WHICH REQUIRES WILLING OBEDIENCE

This brings us to consider the magnificent, perfect example we have in our Lord and Savior, Jesus Christ. As Calvin wrote in his commentary, "The humility to which the Apostle exhorted them in words, he now commends by the example of Christ. There are two parts: In the first, he invites us to imitate Christ because it is the rule of life; in the second, it is the road by which we attain unto glory."

So we read these words once more: "Let this mind be in you which was also in Christ Jesus ..." Paul could have rightly held himself up as a good example in these things, and it would have been true, but rather he lifts up the Lord Jesus as our supreme and truest example of this needed humility as the basis for unity. Then he lists the ways by which our Lord serves as our example of true love, and true humility.

He who always was and always continues to be God, and made it clear to His disciples that He was in His very nature equal with God the Father, saying, "I and the Father are One," and again, "Before Abraham was I Am." So His claim was just and true, but by the Incarnation humbled Himself that He might accomplish our salvation. And how did He humble Himself? Not by subtraction, but by addition. He came into the world, born of a virgin, taking upon Himself a true body and a rational human soul. Though He was perfect and sinless, yet he came into a world as a human who was under the curse of sin, with a body which could be killed, and a heart which could be and often was broken. For, "He suffered under Pontius Pilate, crucified, dead and buried." He took the place of Adam and all his posterity just as if He, not Adam, and we had rebelled and broken everyone of God's commands. Or as Paul said in another place, "He who knew no sin, became sin for us, that we might be made the righteousness of God in Him."

Now, all of this is said at this point to reinforce the call to humility, love, and helpfulness among believers. We are called to look at our hearts, our attitudes and actions which fall so short of this ideal in order that we might repent of our failures and determine to ask, "If my Lord and Savior, Almighty God in human form would do this for me, how can I possibly be unwilling to 'let this mind be also in me' in all my dealings and actions within His body the Church?"

"For by this will all men know that we are His disciples, if we have love for one for another."

Questions for Discussion and Reflection

1. Summarize Paul's instructions for living as a community of faith
    that is of one mind in Christ. What would you look for in your own
    congregation as evidence that these characteristics are present?

2. How does division affect the health of a church community?
    Consider this from three perspectives: (1) witness to the Gospel,
    (2) growth of the community, and (3) the congregation's
    effectiveness both within the church and in the wider community.

3. Consider your own congregation. Does divisiveness exist? If so, in
    what way? What steps are being taken toward healing?

4. What does it mean to be "of one mind"?

5. What does it mean to act with humility?

7

FOLLOWING CHRIST, OUR EXAMPLE
Philippians 2:1-11

There is a great overlooked truth about Christianity which Bible-believing Christians for the most part are simply ignoring. That truth is very simple to state, but exceedingly difficult to fully understand and even more difficult to obey. That truth is this challenge: We are mandated as believers in Jesus Christ to follow Him as our example for living in this world. How many Christians do you know who live like Jesus Christ lived?

At the beginning of the twentieth century, when liberalism began to overwhelm and blot out true and biblical Christianity in most of the mainline churches, there began to be a de-emphasis on the great doctrines concerning the person and work of Jesus Christ. People were not regarded as sinners who need forgiveness and salvation. Quite the contrary, liberalism taught that human nature was basically good and had no need of a crucified and risen Savior. The unique deity of Jesus Christ as God's only begotten Son, conceived by the Holy Spirit and born of the Virgin Mary, was denied. It was generally admitted that He was a great teacher of truth and truly a righteous man, but certainly not the third person of the Trinity who took upon Himself a true body and true human nature. Anything in the New Testament which suggested the supernatural nature of Christ and Christianity was rejected and scorned.

Since according to liberalism we neither had nor needed a Savior from sin, all we really needed was a good example to bring out the best in us. This was the only significance assigned to Jesus Christ. Since He was a good man, then we should be, and indeed can be, good people simply by following His example. In this way, we, too, may become God's sons and daughters and bring the Kingdom of God on earth where all people would be brothers and sisters. This, we were told, would end all human ills. War would be outlawed. There would be no need of prisons. Hunger would give way to prosperity and plenty for all, and by universal public education, mankind was on the verge of solving all its problems and ushering in the golden age people had longed for since the beginning of time.

Of course, biblical Christians rejected this blatant heresy and began to strike back. The full inspiration of all Scripture was ably defended as were the core doctrines of biblical faith. Yes, Jesus Christ was and is the only begotten Son of God, who became a man in just the way the Bible presented. The lost condition of all people apart from Christ was once more proclaimed, and the cross and resurrection became the heart and soul of preaching and teaching again. "Ye must be born again" was proclaimed far and wide.

And because the liberals had so sadly misused the truth that Jesus is our example for living holy lives, that whole idea of looking to Jesus as our example became suspect. This led to the idea now rampant among those identified as Bible-believing, that all that was needed was a "one time decision for Christ." Godly living was of course held up as a good thing, but not absolutely indispensable for being saved.

But if we really want to be true to the whole biblical message and be faithful to our God-sent Savior, we must believe and proclaim that Christ - our Savior from sin through His incarnation, death on the cross, and resurrection from the dead - is also our example for living a life pleasing to God, thus proving our faith is real and saving.

I. FOLLOWING JESUS CHRIST AS OUR EXAMPLE BEGINS BY BELIEVING THE TRUTH ABOUT HIM WHICH GOD HAS REVEALED IN HIS WORD

No one has ever been saved by trying to follow Jesus Christ as an example, but sooner or later every sincere believer will adopt this as his or her own goal for living. It begins by believing the witness of the Bible to Jesus Christ. The Bible declares plainly, and with no apologies, that Jesus Christ was the Son of God from all eternity, and also became a man, being conceived by the Holy Spirit and born of the Virgin Mary. According to the gospels, His life's purpose was to fulfill God's will and to love both his Father and His people with all His heart, strength, and mind. When He had finished His ministry, He went to the cross and died an atoning death, taking upon Himself our sins and accepting the just punishment for them.

According to Scripture, He arose again on the third day, in the same body in which He suffered, and then after forty more days, went back to heaven to await the Father's time to return to the world to bring final judgment, and to receive His people to be with Him in a glorious new heaven and earth. The Bible teaches that whoever believes these things sincerely will be included in that glorious homecoming.

II. FOLLOWING JESUS CHRIST AS OUR EXAMPLE REQUIRES A SERIOUS STUDY OF HIS MIND, HIS HEART, HIS PURPOSES, AND HIS LIFESTYLE

But there is more to being saved than theoretical acceptance of these propositions. Jesus' first words as He began his public ministry were, "repent and believe" and almost His next words, were "follow me." When the Apostle wrote, "Let this mind be in you which was also in Christ Jesus," this was another way of saying what Jesus had said so many times during His earthly ministry.

You don't have to wonder, "What would Jesus do?" That is made very clear in Scripture. In fact, this text summarizes beautifully what it means to have in you the mind of Christ. This speaks of His whole focus of life. He came into the world for one purpose, and that was to do His Father's will and rescue His Father's people. For this, He willingly laid aside His heavenly glory, entered into the world in the most humble way possible, lived a life of complete self-sacrifice, and died a painful and shameful death upon the cross. The purpose for His life lay outside Himself. Long before He went to the cross, He had laid aside all his rights and privileges as the Son of God, and had died to ambition, pride, and earthly fame and power, that He might save those whom the Father had given Him.

He was the only man who had all the rights and privileges we try to claim and cling to, and He gave them all up for us. When you accept Jesus Christ as your Lord and Savior, you are committing yourself to following Him as your example. This means seeking the meaning of life beyond your own pleasure, security, and happiness, and in fact willingly giving up all these things if need be to follow Jesus Christ. I could easily spend the rest of this time, and indeed the rest of this day citing passage after passage from the words of Christ and His apostles which demand that those who profess to believe in Jesus Christ are called upon by God to follow Him as your one and only true example. Remember why believers were called "Christians" in Antioch, and then throughout the world? It was because they were living and conducting themselves like Jesus did.

III. FOLLOWING CHRIST AS OUR EXAMPLE IS THE NORM FOR CHRISTIANS, BUT IT IS BOTH DEMANDING AND PAINFUL

Jesus who said, "Follow me, and I will make you become fishers of men," also said, "If any one desires to come after me, let him deny himself and take up his cross daily and follow me. For whoever desires to save his life will lose it, and whoever loses his life for my sake will save it. For what will it profit a person to gain the whole world and is himself lost or destroyed?"

If you are not laying down all your ambition, your pride, your jealousy, and your self-serving mind at the feet of Jesus, and consciously adopting His mind and disposition, you are not following Him; you are turning your back on Him.

Oh yes, come to Bethlehem and see the Christ Child. Hear the angels sing, huddle with the shepherds around the fire in the open fields near the manger, walk with the wisemen in their search for the newborn King. But oh, best beloved, please know that when we name

Him as our Lord and Savior, we are making a commitment to live
a new kind of life and be at odds with the world around us. We are
committing ourselves to His cross, being crucified with Him, that the
dying of Jesus may be made manifest in our lives. Don't linger too
long at the manger looking at a baby, a wondrous baby to be sure;
but rather gaze long and linger a lifetime at the cross, for there you
will discover the means of your salvation, and there you will discover
that the Christ who died there for you calls upon you to lay down
your life for His sake, and the sake of those for whom he died.

It was not until after our Lord humbled Himself and became a
servant, becoming obedient unto death on a shameful cross, that
God raised Him from the dead and exalted Him to heaven's highest
throne. And it is not until you follow Him as your Savior and
example that you will share in that same glory and assurance.

Not too many years after the Emancipation Proclamation, freeing
all the slaves, an old black man who had been born a slave and had
fled north to freedom decided to go back to Georgia where he was
born that he might die among his own people. He worked long and
hard to earn enough money for a ticket to fulfill his purpose. When
the conductor came through the car calling for tickets, a young
white woman tearfully explained to the conductor that she had no
ticket, but had received word her husband was in a dying condition
in Georgia and she was trying to reach him before he died. The
conductor said he was sorry, but if he let her ride he would lose his
job. So he told her she would have to get off the train at the next
stop. As the train slowed for that stop, the old white haired black
man stepped to her side and simply said, "Here's your ticket to
Georgia ma'am." So he was put off the train in her stead. The last
anyone ever saw of him, he was trudging slowly along with bowed

head, bent back, and a shabby little suitcase, trying to walk those hundreds of miles so he could die among his own people. I never heard if he made it or not, I hope he did, but I'm very sure he was welcomed home by Another who gave up His place and life that others might live. "Let this mind be in you which was also in Christ Jesus."

Questions for Discussion and Reflection

1. Discuss the great flaw of liberalism in terms of its view of the person of Jesus. Why is this view dangerous?

2. Why is a "one-time decision for Christ" insufficient for living a life that is truly faithful to our Savior? What is required in order to truly follow Christ as our example?

3. What does it mean to deny yourself and take up your cross daily?

8

GOD HIGHLY
EXALTED HIM
Philippians 2:1-11

"God highly exalted Him and has given Him the name which is above all names; that at the name of Jesus, every knee should bow, of those in heaven, and of those on earth, and of those under the earth, and that every tongue should confess that Jesus Christ is Lord, to the glory of God the Father."

If the story of Christmas ends at the manger in Bethlehem, it is but a beautiful, winsome, and meaningless tale. If it ends at the cross, it is a travesty and a testimony that life is a tale that has been told, full of sound and fury and signifying nothing. But Christmas does not end in Bethlehem, or even at the cross. Christmas ends where it began: with Jesus Christ, God's beloved and only begotten Son, at the Father's right hand, given all power and authority in heaven and on earth, the object of worship and homage.

In Advent 2003, I began a sermon series on Philippians 2:1-11 with the appeal, "Let this mind be in you which was also in Christ Jesus" – a call to believers to take seriously the call to pattern our lives after Jesus Christ. Over the next weeks, we traced the pattern of redemption as seen in these verses; how our Lord, who in His essential nature was one with the Father and fully God from all eternity, willingly humbled Himself and became obedient unto the death of the cross for our sakes. Then, we came to the glorious and thrilling climax of this story as we read: "Therefore, God also has highly exalted Him and given Him the name which is above every name, that at the name of Jesus every knee should bow ... and every tongue should confess that Jesus Christ is Lord, to the glory of God the Father." Without these words, Christmas would be incomplete, and we should be left without hope.

Since God is God, this had to happen. Since a just and holy God rules and overrules in the story of mankind, the Lord Jesus Christ had to be vindicated and glorified. Since the Scripture – the Word of God – is true, the Savior who came into the world, and suffered and died for our sins, must be lifted up, restored, and enthroned as King of kings, and Lord of lords. Let's try to understand what this means, both for Him and for us.

I.   GOD HIGHLY EXALTED HIM

Jesus said, "Whoever humbles himself will be exalted." He is the supreme example of this glorious and saving truth. He humbled himself, and therefore God the Father highly exalted Him.

Yes, we who are willing to humble ourselves under the mighty hand of God, confess our unworthiness and sin, will one day be both exonerated and exalted in God's good time. But there is a vast difference between our exaltation and that of our Lord Jesus. It is true that the Bible uses the same verb to describe believers' exaltation and that of our Lord. BUT in this passage, a verb is used that is used in no other place in the New Testament, and it is applied only to our Lord Jesus. That is why our translation reads. "... God HIGHLY EXALTED Him," and even that fails to fully satisfy the meaning of this word. It is exaltation to the superlative degree. It means God lifted Him up to the highest possible position of honor and adoration.

Yes, the Bible teaches that believers go to heaven to be with the Lord forever, but of Jesus it is said, "He passed through the heavens" and "was lifted high above the heavens" and "ascended far above the all the heavens." This means He was given the highest place of honor and glory, and is seated at the right hand of God's throne." "Far above all rule and authority and power and dominion, and every name that is named, not only in this age, but in that which is to come."

All of this happened as the prophets foretold. See the justice of God displayed in Christ's exaltation. On earth, He was condemned as a law breaker and blasphemer, but the Father said of Him, "No, He is My Son, and in Him I am well pleased." The earth judged Him, the Father appointed Him the judge of all people. He who became poor for my sake has now again become the richest of the rich. The Savior rejected by the world has been fully accepted both in His person and in His work. He who had to learn obedience through suffering has been given all authority and all power in heaven and on earth. He who was reduced to the poorest peasantry in His birth, life, and death, has become the glorious Prophet, Priest, and King.

II. GOD HAS GIVEN HIM THE NAME ABOVE ALL NAMES

It was said by the prophets of old that Messiah would be given the highest name above all names. In the words of inspired Isaiah, "He will be called Immanuel, God with us." Or again: "For unto us a child is born. Unto us a Son is given, and the government shall be upon His shoulders, and His name shall be called: Wonderful Counselor, Mighty God, Everlasting Father, the Prince of Peace." These titles were His by right when He came into the world, but He laid aside all the glory and honor of that name until the Father exalted Him in the glory of the resurrection and ascension. Now these names have been bestowed upon Him and can never be laid aside again. Truly, Jesus is the name above all names.

Look more closely at Isaiah's words about our Lord. He did not say His name shall be called Emmanuel as a symbol that God is with us. He simply said His name shall be called Emmanuel, God with us. It was the virgin-born Son who himself was and is God with us.

Isaiah did not write of the child to be born, and the son to be given, that He would be a sign that God is a wonderful counselor, the mighty God, the everlasting Father, the Prince of Peace. No, he wrote of this coming child and son, HIS name shall be called Wonderful Counselor, etc.

Isaiah uses some of the most impressive names for God Himself to tell us who this coming child shall be. But Isaiah did not speak for himself. He was a prophet of God, who only spoke words given to him. Of these words, like all he wrote, he could say, "Thus saith the Lord."

So, the great name which encompasses all these lofty, exalted titles, and far more, was bestowed on Jesus by the Father Himself. If you think Jesus of Nazareth was less than this, you are calling God a liar.

III. GOD HAS DECREED THAT ALL CREATION AND ALL CREATURES WILL BOW AND CONFESS THAT JESUS CHRIST IS LORD, TO THE GLORY OF THE FATHER

When the Bible says, "Every knee should bow and every tongue should confess that Jesus Christ is Lord," this includes all created beings: angels in heaven and people on earth and all who have ever lived. Holy angels and redeemed people will do this with great joy and glad adoration. Fallen angels and all people who are condemned because of unbelief and rejection of God's Son will confess to their doom that He is Lord because they that have despised and rejected Him.

Listen as the blessed adore and worship Him as recorded at Revelation 5:8-14. Listen also as the condemned also confess Him, as found at Revelation 6:12-17. This all brings us to a burning question which demands an answer from everyone who hears. Since God has exalted Jesus Christ, (who humbled Himself by being born as a man, living a life of self-sacrifice and poverty, dying a cruel, shameful death on a Roman cross) and given Him the Name above all names, and decreed that all must and will confess Him--in which of these two multitudes are you numbered even now? In which will you be found on that day of final vindication of the Lord Jesus? Among His followers, or among all who have rejected Him and await condemnation? This question urgently demands an answer from each and every heart.

Questions for Discussion and Reflection

1. Revisit the words of Isaiah as discussed in this chapter. Discuss the specific nature of the language, i.e., that the Child is not a sign; rather, the Child is, etc. Delve into the truth that this conveys.

2. Is there a relationship between Jesus' humiliation and His exaltation? What is it?

3. What is the difference between our promised exaltation and Christ's exaltation?

9

HE HUMBLED HIMSELF
Philippians 2:1-11

Have you ever thought what might have happened if God had appointed a committee to decide how His Son would come into the world? Why, of course there would be a spectacular celebration. There would be a shower of shooting stars, mighty thundering in the heavens. Ten thousand times ten thousand of heaven's most beautiful and awesome angels would announce His coming. The great and mighty of the world would be assembled to greet and welcome Him. He would come in the form of a mighty conquering hero, whom no one dared oppose. Tribute would be brought to Him from earth's farthest ends. He would be arrayed in costly silks and resplendent robes befitting His lofty estate.

The Reverend Harry Schutte, one-time minister of church growth for our presbytery, had a sign on his desk which read, "For God so loved the world that He did not send a committee." Amen!

You know that the exact opposite of these things happened when God sent His Son Jesus into the world. No vast shower of shooting stars, but one bright star which led wise men from the east to Bethlehem. There were no thunder blasts roaring. Only one angel, who came to a peasant girl named Mary to tell her that she would conceive in her womb, by the Holy Spirit, and that the child born of her would be the Son of the Highest. Later, one angel proclaimed the good news of the Savior's birth "to certain poor shepherds in the fields as they lay keeping their sheep on a cold winter's night that was so deep."

When the wise men came to Jerusalem and told their story to mighty Herod, his only reaction was an attempt to murder the child, and although he failed to kill the infant Jesus, he did manage to kill all the little boys in and around Bethlehem. God's Son did not come in the form of a mighty hero whom all would fear, but as a tiny, helpless baby whom none could fear. Nor was He arrayed in costly silks and crimson robes, but was wrapped in swaddling clothes and laid in a manger because there was no room in the village inn.

That's how God in His wisdom, and without the help of a committee, sent His beloved Son into the world. And the mighty Creator Son, who was in the essential nature with the Father and through whom the Father made all things, humbled himself past all imagination and entered the world. THAT He came and HOW He came are so intertwined as to be inseparable. Only God in His wisdom could have arranged His birth so perfectly.

I. HE HUMBLED HIMSELF IN HIS BIRTH

Christ humbled Himself in His birth, not only by what He gave up, but by what He became. It was not by subtraction, but by addition.

When He laid aside His heavenly glory, it was not by ceasing to be God, but by also becoming a man for our poor sakes. That's how He humbled Himself. It would have been humility enough for the King of Creation, the Creator, to be willing to be born to the mightiest king of this world, or even to the High Priest. But for Him to be born of the poorest and lowliest of people was His way of showing that He had come to save the poor and the lowly of earth. Were you born a wee baby? So was He. Were you born in poverty and want? So was He. Did you endure hardship and danger? So did He, even as a little baby boy. Are there some who look down on you? All looked down on Him. Shepherds and other poor people, must you wrap your new-born in swaddling clothes? So His mother wrapped him at birth, for that's all she had.

Shortly after I was born (at home because my parents couldn't afford a hospital), Mother and Daddy lost almost everything they had in the Great Depression, which made paupers out of many. When their business failed, they lost the new home they had built a few years before, most of their furniture, china, and silver. They lost their car and Dad's fleet of trucks he used in his business. They moved into a two-room upstairs apartment with five children, living in poverty and uncertainty. When at last my father regained his former position as a forest ranger, after being unemployed for six months, he was sent far from home and told to get there the best way he could, which was on a freight train headed west. Mother was left with five small children, and nothing much more.

But when Jesus was born, it was in a borrowed barn, his bed a feed trough. When He was but eight-days-old, He was taken to the temple in Jerusalem to receive the covenantal sign of cleansing, circumcision, though He was without any sin at all. At forty days,

He was taken again for the ceremony of Mary's cleansing and to be devoted to the Lord as the first-born male of the family. An offering was to be given by the parents, usually a lamb, but for the very poor, two doves were the acceptable sacrifice. That was all Joseph could give, for He was but a poor carpenter and at that time unemployed. The only transportation His parents could afford was walking, and possibly a donkey for Mary.

Joseph was warned by an angel and the royal family fled by night into a foreign land, there to live as migrants Jesus' first few years on earth. That's the story of His birth. "No drums astir, no trumpet sounds were heard when to His own He came. Only sleeping beasts in their stalls and Mary whispering His name."

II. HE HUMBLED HIMSELF IN HIS LIFE

It was not only in the circumstance of His birth that God the Son humbled Himself, but also in the life He lived for thirty-three years. He grew up in Nazareth, a town looked down on by most. The name in Hebrew means "branch," and the prophet Isaiah said that when Messiah came He would be "a branch from the root of David." When He was being praised as a prophet by some early in His ministry, the religious leaders laughed at the idea and asked, "Can any good thing come out of Nazareth?"

His early years were as the son of a poor carpenter, and apparently both He and His mother were the objects of gossip because of His conception before marriage. That he was conceived by the Holy Spirit, and was the Son of God, was beyond the understanding of most, and believed by only Mary and Joseph.

When He began His public ministry, it was not as the high priest in the temple, though He was the only true high priest who has ever lived. But He appeared on the scene as a traveling rabbi, who had but a small following of twelve men and a few faithful women. By His teaching and many miracles, He attracted a large following at first, but most soon faded away. He was accorded little if any honor either in the temple or in the synagogues He visited. When one eager would-be disciple said, "Master, I will follow you wherever you go," Jesus responded, "The birds of the air have their nests, and the foxes of the fields have their dens, but the Son of Man has nowhere to lay His head."

Have you ever been weary, hungry, and thirsty? So has He. Have you ever been disappointed in God's people and felt let down by those you trusted. So has He. "What? Could you not watch and pray with me one hour," He asked his three most trusted disciples. Have you been sorely tempted when you were weak? So was He.

That was the story of His short life on earth. He humbled Himself and lived a life of self-sacrifice and service. When He met with His disciples in the upper room to celebrate the Passover, there was no servant there to stoop down and wash their feet, so humbly and willingly He took that role, girding Himself with a towel and washed their feet. But even when he was dressed as a common servant and did a servant's duty, He was still God, who had humbled Himself to become our Savior.

I am reminded of Damien, the leper priest of Hawaii, who entered the leper colony knowing he was forfeiting his own life and health to care for the dying lepers on that lonely island. But our Savior came down from a much higher place to a much lower place when He humbled Himself. And He suffered more terribly than even brave, good Damien.

III. HE HUMBLED HIMSELF IN HIS DEATH

But it was supremely in His death that He completely humbled Himself. He was the Lord and giver of life, but he tasted death for all His beloved. When our text tells us, "He humbled Himself," it goes right on to say "and became obedient unto death, EVEN THE DEATH OF THE CROSS!"

Do you realize our Lord Jesus, who had never done one thing wrong in all His life, but freely gave Himself in loving service to any and all who sought His aid, was accused of the worst possible crimes, tried illegally, tortured in the process, and was finally condemned as if He was one of the worst criminals?

His death was painful and shameful. The historians of Rome, especially Cicero, tell us that only the most vile, wicked slaves who committed unspeakable crimes were ever executed in this way. So, in official Roman records, Jesus of Nazareth was a wicked, vile sinner who deserved the worst possible form of death.

Look at Him there on the cross, writhing in anguish and pain, reviled and mocked by Romans and Jews, rejected by the crowds He had served so unselfishly, deserted by His few friends, and terribly punished inwardly with the fires of hell burning His soul, forsaken by His Father.

When He looked upon you with love and mercy, He sealed His own fate, but He did it knowing what would happen to Him, and He did it willingly.

That is why we have Christmas; and that is why I unashamedly beg you with all my heart and soul to love Jesus with all your heart and soul, and walk willingly in His steps, saying, "Let this mind be in you which was also in Christ Jesus." Is that asking too much?

Questions for Discussion and Reflection

1. Re-read the scripture passage (Phil. 2:1-11). Talk about the significance of Jesus being equal with God. What did Jesus leave behind to become a man and give His life on a cross for our sin?

2. In what ways did Jesus take on the nature of a servant?

3. We are called to be of one mind with each other in Christ. How does humility play into the role of serving others?

4. One way in which Jesus demonstrated his humility was by obedience to the Father. How does obedience to God demonstrate our humility?

10

THE MIND OF CHRIST
Philippians 2:1-11

"Let this mind be in you which was also in Christ Jesus. Who, being in the form of God; did not consider it robbery to be equal with God..." (Phil. 2:5-6) Or, as John wrote, "The Word was with God, the Word was God."

When I was a young boy living in the little village of Weaverville, North Carolina, there was a woman in our community who taught music in the public schools. She conducted the glee clubs, taught kids to play band instruments, piano, organ, and voice lessons. She worked long and hard to teach a bunch of high school kids to sing Handel's Messiah, spending untold hours working with each section so we could learn the intricate harmony of that great music. She was one of the most talented musicians and teachers I have ever known. Of course, then we took Miss Irene for granted. After all, she had been born and raised in the mountain town and everyone knew her folks. So why shouldn't she spend her life there and do all these things?

What I didn't know for a long time was she had been educated to the master's level in one of the most prestigious universities and music conservatories in the United States. She was widely sought after and could have been a well-known and even famous musician in several different fields of music, including a very beautiful soprano voice. But out of love for her people and town, she gave all that up and instead poured her life into making music lovers and God lovers out of many children, teenagers, and adults. It was not until I discovered who she really was, and could have been, that I appreciated those long hours, days, and years of unappreciated work in my behalf and many others like me.

Later, when I was a home mission pastor in the Cumberland Mountains of east Tennessee, there was another mountain preacher who would come and preach revival services for us almost every year. Preacher Franklin was a wonderful, spirit-filled man, with unique gifts and great power in spite of his homespun ways. Though I appreciated and loved to hear him preach, it was not until later I learned he was one of the most sought-after preachers in the whole country. He had preached in some of the largest and most prestigious churches all over this land, and time after time had been offered the call to become pastor of large and wealthy churches. I doubt if the people in those little churches up in Farner, Tellico Plains, or Madison, Tennessee understood any more than I did what a great and famous man he was who lived among them and unselfishly poured out his life serving God's people in small and humble places. Hold onto these stories, and they may help you understand what I will now try to convey to you about Christ and Christmas.

The call to believers to follow the example of Christ, especially in His incredible humility, is an irresistible call only if you consider, and to some degree understand, the words of this text: "Christ Jesus, being in the form of God, did not consider it robbery to be equal with God..."

You must start right here if you want to understand and appreciate the meaning of the Incarnation (that Jesus, the Son of God, took on human flesh). If you cannot fully believe and embrace this truth, you will never really understand what Christmas is all about.

Just a quick note about that one expression, "being in the form of God." Several prominent cults play on these words to try to prove that Jesus was not really God; He was just in the form of God. But that position ignores the meaning of the word 'form' as it is used here. The word in the original language in this context means 'essential nature', pointing to the underlying reality of Christ's identity as God the Son. Now, if this was the only place in all the Bible in which it was affirmed that Jesus Christ is truly God, then we might look again at this expression, but this verse has to be understood in light of the overwhelming number of passages which teach the full deity of our Lord Jesus Christ. It was no big deal if He was just another man, no matter how holy and good. But if the Old Testament prophecies are true, if the claims of Christ Himself are real, if the testimony of those who knew Him best is valid, He was not just another man, holy and good. He was the eternal God in the person of His eternal Son, who eternally pre-existed in the very nature of God. This is what makes the Christian faith absolutely unique, and it is what makes our Christmas joy overwhelmingly glorious and life-changing.

Ever so briefly, review with me the several statements which leave no doubt that the writers of the Bible, both Old and New testaments, clearly believed that Jesus the Messiah was actually God.

I. THE OLD TESTAMENT WITNESS

I cannot begin to cite all the many passages concerning Christ in which the prophets of old clearly expected the coming Messiah would be truly God, but listen as I quote these words from Isaiah. "Behold! The virgin shall conceive and bear a son, and thou shall call His name Emmanuel, GOD with us." And again, "For unto us a child is born, unto us a son is given. And the government shall be upon His shoulders. And His name shall be called, Wonderful Counselor, Mighty God, Everlasting Father, Prince of peace." Micah said the child born in Bethlehem would be the one whose days were from all eternity, and that can only be the eternal God!

No mortal man fulfills such lofty ascriptions of power and glory. Unless these inspired writers were wrong in their assumptions, when Messiah came, He would be the LORD Himself.

II. THE CONFIRMATION OF THE NEW TESTAMENT

When the angel Gabriel told the frightened young Virgin Mary she would have a baby, who would be the Messiah, he said: "Do not be afraid, Mary, for you have found favor with God, and behold you will conceive in your womb and bring forth a Son, and shall call His name Jesus. He shall be great, and be called the Son of the Highest; and the Lord God will give Him the throne of His father, David. And He shall reign over the house of Jacob forever, and of His kingdom, there shall be no end."

Now hear what John said of Him. "In the beginning was the Word, and the Word was with GOD, and the Word was GOD. All things were made through Him, and without Him nothing was made that was made. He came into the world, and the world was made though Him."

These passages teach remarkable things about the One true God. (1) The mighty, one God exists in three persons: the Father, the Son, and the Holy Spirit. (2) These three persons are one God, the same in substance and equal in power and glory. (3) It was through the power of that second Person all that creation came into being.

Of the many words of Paul affirming the full deity of Christ, aside from the text from Philippians, the one which states the case most clearly is found in Galatians 4:4: "But when the fullness of time had come, God sent forth His Son, born of a woman, born under the law."

III. THE IMPORTANCE AND MEANING OF THIS GREAT TRUTH

Just how important is it for us to understand this incredible truth? Do you want to be a true Christian? Do you want to really know Jesus Christ? Do you want to have your sins forgiven? Do you want to go to heaven when you die? All these sought-for blessings rest on this foundational truth: Jesus Christ is God's Son and just as truly God as the Father Himself.

So, when we celebrate Christmas and receive all the joy and wonder God intends for you to experience, we must begin by understanding that the little tiny baby born in Bethlehem was from all eternity the great God through whom the Father created all things, including mankind in His image. To know and appreciate the Gospel in all its saving power, you must know that the baby conceived in the womb of the Virgin Mary, cradled in her arms and nursing at her breast, was God the Son in human flesh and nature.

He came from the highest throne of heaven to the lowliest place on earth, a manger in a stable. Everyone in Heaven, the glorious angels included, knew who He was and constantly sang His praise and worshiped Him unceasingly. But no one on earth seemed to fully know who He was, even His believing mother and His closest disciples. They always seemed amazed at the things He was able to do, but never quite grasped until after His death and resurrection that He really was God's Son, one with the Father and Holy Spirit.

His mother expected miracles of Him, but at one point wanted to take Him home because she thought He had lost His mind. When the frightened disciples saw Him stand up in the boat on that storm-tossed sea and speak the words, "Peace be still," they watched in awe as the wind ceased and instantly the waves calmed. "Who is this," they whispered, "that even the wind and waves obey Him?" But when they saw Him in His glorious resurrection power, their own question was answered. "Truly this man is the Son of God!"

Do you understand, maybe even a little bit, how wonderful this is? Why, yes, He can forgive your sins. He can give you peace on your storm-tossed sea. He can make you right with God and give you His power to live a life pleasing to God. He can comfort you in your deepest distress and point your downcast eyes towards the skies. He can raise you from the dead and acquit you on the judgment day. He can wipe away all your bitter tears, take away your pain and grief, and cleanse you from all sin. He can open before you an eternity of fulfillment, joy, and peace.

How can He do all this? Because He was and is God. And in the Bethlehem event, He became also man, bonding Him both to the Father in heaven and to us in our lowly and lost estate. And to this very day and forever and ever, He remains both God and man in one person with two distinct natures: our Savior, and our Lord God.

No, I didn't really appreciate Miss Irene or Preacher Franklin until at last I understood what they gave up to do what they did for me and many others. Nor do I or you fully appreciate Jesus Christ until you understand all He gave up to come into this world, born in Bethlehem's manger, dying on Calvary's cross as our sin-bearer. But when you begin to see who He was before coming into the world, your heart and mind can scarcely take it in, and you want to kneel before His manger, cross, and throne, and crown Him Lord of All. Don't you? Won't you, even now?

Questions for Discussion and Reflection

1. Discuss the meaning of the phrase, "being in the form of God." Keep in mind the meaning of the word 'form' in the original language ('essential nature').

2. Ponder the timeline of the Incarnation to the Ascension: Christ, co-equal with the Father, before being born as man; His birth into poverty; His servanthood; His ministry of teaching, preaching, healing; His passion, death, and resurrection; His ascension back into heaven. Now, journal or discuss the enormity of this event and – in light of all you have discovered   through Paul's letter to the Philippians – (1) how it is intertwined with your life and (2) how you must live into it.

11

REPENTING OF THE TERRIBLE SIN OF PRIDE
Philippians 2:1-11

One of the great Christian minds of our generation or any other, and certainly one of the great Christians of our time, is Dr. James I. Packer. He was on campus at Reformed Theological Seminary in Jackson, Mississippi, lecturing and preaching when I was on the faculty. The powers then asked me to take Dr. Packer to lunch one day, which I was most happy to do. This meant I could spend a little time in the presence of this man whom I admire so much and from whom I have learned a great deal. Being proper and respectful around this spiritual giant came quite naturally for me, and as we dined and visited together I of course addressed him as Dr. Packer. About the third time I did this he tried to put me at ease by saying, in his gracious and inimitable way, "Gordon, why don't you just call me James, or even Jim." I was so taken back by his kindness and his humility, I replied, "Very well, Jim, and you may call me Dr. Reed."

When Dr. Duncan assigned me responsibility of preaching on ministerial repentance, my first thought was that this is going to be a really long sermon, because I must first list all the sins from which I need to repent. After a good half hour of going over the list, I decided to group all these things into categories, but I was still in the half-hour bracket, and not even to the point of saying why and how one should repent of these many evils. So, it became obvious that further reduction in the miserable catalog of ministerial sins would be necessary. In fact, I have reduced it to one, the one most common and surely most hideous in God's sight, and the most destructive of true ministry in the lives of God's chosen. I speak, of course, of pride. Pride is bred within our fallen nature, but the most productive soil in which it may be found, and in which it grows most abundantly and with its deepest roots, is in the hearts and lives of ministers in the Church of Jesus Christ. Not only is it common among those of us called to be ministers in His Church, but it is, to our great shame, the most un-Christ-like attitude one might ever imagine. As an example, the only way we have been able to encourage ministers to pursue even a limited amount of continuing education is to call it a Doctor of Ministry degree.

Many, many passages of Scripture would serve to give a biblical underpinning to this message, and my greatest problem was not finding a passage to exposit and from which to fervently exhort. The most difficult decision was simply this: which section of the Word should I choose? There are so many which deal with this terrible sin of pride, both in the form of precept and by example.

I. THE INITIAL EXHORTATION

This passage from the second chapter of Philippians is the one to which the Holy Spirit seemed to be nudging me most pressingly.

There are some interesting theological difficulties here, and the devil will do everything he possibly can to keep your attention and focus on other things. For unless you recognize the power and control of this sin, sincerely repent of it, and become a power for the Lord, you will pay little mind to the central theme which protects your heart against any unsettling conviction.

I recognize immediately that the word 'pride' itself is not used here, but certainly in the words, "empty conceit" and "vainglory," we have two synonyms for that word. In fact, by dictionary definition, 'vainglory' means 'ostentatious pride,' and conceit means having an excessively high opinion of oneself or abilities. When you combine the word 'empty' with 'conceit', you add to the sin of pride, and poor judgment as well.

As the chapter begins with the Apostle's appeal, based on the abundant blessings which are ours in Christ, there is at least a suggestion that maybe all was not well within the congregation of believers. One gets the feeling that they, like us, had let slip the wonder of those blessings received as a result of their fellowship in Christ and with each other. So, he enumerates them again by way of reminder. In Christ, and in the goodly fellowship with each other, they had received encouragement, consolation, love, fellowship of the Holy Spirit, affection and compassion. Since they had experienced these blessings, he then appealed to them to make his joy complete by maintaining that unity, love, and single mindedness inherent in their common bond of faith.

Of course, commitment to that precious unity requires that nothing be done in empty conceit and vainglory, but with humility of mind and a mutual esteem and love that builds up the brothers rather than tearing them down.

But what this passage is really all about is a powerful call for believers to experience and sincerely demonstrate the opposite of pride, which is humility. If pride is the besetting sin of the ministry and the foundation for all sorts of other sins, then humility is that rarest of all virtues, the most desirable and Christ-like of all, and the foundation for all other virtues required in Christ's body.

II. JESUS CHRIST'S AMAZING EXAMPLE OF HUMILITY

The Holy Spirit in His wisdom well knows that simple command, or even fervent exhortation, would not be enough to crack the shell of pride in which we, turtle-like, are bound. Only the lifting up of the truly amazing example of our Lord Jesus Christ's incredible display of humility from conception to crucifixion would be sufficient for such a difficult to impossible undertaking. Take notice, dear brothers, Paul never hesitated to point to the Lord Jesus as our supreme example for all goodness and virtues. Somehow, those of us who identify as evangelical and reformed preachers seem loathed to preach on Christ as our example, lest we might imply salvation by example rather than by atonement. But if Christ is not also our example, then faith is barren and orthodoxy is dead, as Dr. Hendrickson observed in his commentary.

He begins by saying, "Let this mind be in you which was also in Christ Jesus", and then shows us where this mind of Christ Jesus took Him. To understand His amazing humility, we must first recognize His true deity, His equality with the Father, being the same in substance and equal in power and glory. "In the form of God" is simply a way of underscoring His complete and essential deity. Yet, He did not consider that His deity, His essential equality with the Father, something which would prevent Him from becoming the suffering servant, and even the Lamb of God who takes away the sin of the world.

You don't need me to point out when the Apostle tells us, "He emptied Himself," this does not mean he ceased to be what He had always been, God the Son, the great Logos, by whom all things were made. No, He did not empty himself by subtraction, but by addition. We adamantly deny the contention of some cults, including liberalism, that at any point, including His conception in the Virgin Mary's womb, He ever deprived Himself of His position in the eternal Godhead.

Nevertheless, He did truly humble Himself in every sense of the word by taking to Himself true humanity in the likeness of fallen humanity with all its weaknesses and woes; though being without sin even in His human nature. As such, He became obedient up to and including His death on the cross.

Here I would pause and look more closely at all this humiliation entailed as a prelude to the injunction laid on us by the Apostle, that we too might "let this mind be also in us."

The humiliation and the humility of Christ is seen in every step of the Incarnation, beginning with His conception by the Holy Spirit in the womb of the young peasant virgin, Mary, the betrothed of Joseph. What condescension! What self-emptying! His humility is displayed on every page of His life's story as we have it in the Gospel. Imagine. The Lord of glory growing up in the home of humble parents and submitting to them, even when they failed to understand that He had to be about His Father's business.

You know the story of His poverty, hardships, fasting, sleepless nights, temptations, accusations of ungodliness by ungodly men and spiritually blind men. You recall the insults, the ridicule, and the mockery He endured. Who can forget the sham of supposed trials mingled with face slapping, spitting, beard pulling, and inane interrogation, the so-called conviction of blasphemy, the crown of thorns and lashing, the cowardice of Pilate, and the hatred of His accusers. Then, of course, there was the demeaning execution on the cross as a common criminal.

I was re-reading the story of His suffering not long ago. I began to be overwhelmed emotionally as I read these things again. My heart was sore, and my eyes were filled with tears. Then I read how the execution squad took His clothes, meager though they were, and which they had stripped from off His beaten body, and divided them among themselves, and at last gambling for the one thing He owned which might have been of some value, His cloak; probably the same one He had laid aside at the last supper in order to wash His disciples' feet. When the awful scene of His degradation filled my mind and heart, I broke down and wept bitterly. They took every last thing He owned. They stripped Him of clothing and dignity, and as He writhed in anguish and pain they mocked Him and dared Him to save Himself. "Let THIS mind be in you that was also in Christ Jesus ..."

But I won't have it so. I am offended if anyone deprives me of what is "rightfully mine." I am angered by the indifference of others to my imagined brilliance and superior spirituality. I am resentful of those who do not pay me proper respect. I am hurt by the slight of friends and the unjust criticism of foes. He prayed, "Father forgive them", while I look for subtle ways of "getting even" with those whom I think may have done me wrong.

I guess what I am trying so poorly to say is that there is only one cure for the terrible sin of pride, and that is to ask, seek, and knock for the gracious, self-forgetting humility of the Lord whom I profess to serve. For how may I possibly preach a Crucified Savior, if I "who belong to Christ" HAVE NOT "crucified the flesh." (Gal. 5:24)

I started out to preach a sermon; I have ended up confessing my sin and exposing my sinful heart. Yet, I hear His blessed voice. He tells me, "As many as I love, I reprove and discipline. Be zealous therefore and repent. Behold, I stand at the door and knock. If anyone hears my voice and opens the door, I will come in to him and dine with him, and he with me." The Lord who humbled Himself so completely in every way, knocks on the heart door of a proud man who calls himself a minister of Christ but is reluctant to humble himself in any way. If I will hear His voice and open the door, He will come in and dine with me and I with Him, and by this my proud spirit will be humbled, my pride broken.

"Lord if you will, you can make me clean." "I will, be thou clean." Amen.

Questions for Discussion and Reflection

1. What does it mean that Christ "emptied himself"?

2. How can you empty yourself of you?

3. What impact does pride have on our actions and decision-making process?

4. Contrast a life of humility versus a life couched in pride. What effect does each have on the health of a faith community?

5. In what areas of your life do you see pride taking control? What can you do to address it?

6. What kind of sermon does your life preach?

12

WORK OUT YOUR
OWN SALVATION
Philippians 2:12-18

Was Paul really a closet Arminian? Is that why he wrote these words? That conclusion would only be reached by a person who ignores the axiom, "A text without a context is a pretext." First, we need to look very carefully at what is actually said, then set it in the context of the entire chapter, book, and the sum total of biblical theology as it is articulated by Paul in his several letters. After citing the example of Christ's willingness to "empty Himself" and demonstrating what this sacrifice cost Him, Paul then tells us how the Father exalted Him and gave Him a name which is above every name, and the promise of subjection to Him by the whole creation.

I. THE PERSONAL APPEAL

This takes us to the text before us which begins with these personal and appealing words: "So then my beloved, even as you have always obeyed, not as in my presence only, but now much more in my absence, work out your own salvation with fear and trembling." The real test of the effectiveness of Paul's past ministry will be the willingness and the ability of this Philippian congregation to continue to walk with the Lord, and to grow in grace and obedience in the absence of their great leader and guide, Paul. I have always contended that the true test of any man's ministry is what happens in a body of believers after he leaves for another field, or is called home by the Lord.

It would seem that Paul was well aware of the esteem in which he was held by this congregation, even as they recognized the great love he had for them. Is there possibly a hint in these words of Paul that just maybe they had been too dependent upon him? By the words, "so then my beloved," Paul reminds the Church in Philippi of the bond of love which still exists between them and their former pastor. He also makes reference to their devoted and loyal following of Christ when he was among them as their pastor. "Even as you have always obeyed" is his commendation. While he was among them, he could bear witness to their love and loyalty to Christ and to the Word which he preached among them. The love between a pastor and a congregation is truly a beautiful thing, and faithfully following Christ is even more beautiful but should never depend on their loyalty to any particular pastor.

So, he exhorts them to exercise their loyalty even more in his absence from them. I remember years ago leaving a congregation in Atlanta and an article written in the church newsletter by the chairman of the Board of Deacons to the congregation. He began his article by saying, "We don't need Gordon Reed at Wee Kirk Covenant Presbyterian Church, [rather, they should depend on the Lord] and I thank him for it" [thanking Gordon for teachng them so]. If I have ever appreciated words of commendation more, I don't know what they would be.

One of the most impressive things about the ministry of Paul was that he always seemed to work towards the end that the congregations he served would depend on the Lord and His Word, and not on him. The most impressive example of this is found in 1 Corinthians 2, where he explained why his preaching was not with persuasive words of man's wisdom, but in demonstration of the Spirit and of power that their faith would not rest in the wisdom of men, but in the power of God. (May it ever be, dear Lord!)

II. THE APOSTOLIC EXHORTATION

Now come these often misunderstood words, but words we dare not neglect, ignore, or misunderstand. "Work out your own salvation with fear and trembling." Now, let's try to understand this as Paul meant it. In the first place, they must mature to the point that without the assistance of Paul, they must work these things out for themselves. The precious gift of faith by grace must be put to work in their lives, showing itself clearly by growing sanctification and the obvious evidence of the fruit of the Spirit, because it is "by their fruits you will know them," according to the words of Jesus. So what's on the inside of you must work outside, as in "let your light so shine before men that they may see your good works and glorify your Father who is in heaven."

Paul's use of the verb tense reinforces the meaning of the text. What he has in mind is a process that is on-going, continuous, and sustained, and indeed very hard work. In this passage, the work of salvation is more closely associated with this growing sanctification than it is with justification. Both are a part of salvation and both the work of grace. In this process of sanctification, believers are not passive, but in every part of Scripture we are urged to press on, to run well the race, fight the good fight, pursue, seek, none of which terms suggest a lazy indifferent attitude nor the position that since salvation is a gift we just "let go and let God." Anytime I hear that song, I always hope it is not being sung by the driver of a car I'm in while traveling down the Blue Ridge Parkway.

In Ephesians, Paul talks about putting on the whole armor of God in order to fight the good fight against the world, the flesh, and the devil. Here, he speaks of the work involved in overcoming and demonstrating by our lives who we are and whose we are. What are some of the practical, everyday ways we must work out our salvation? We all know and profess to believe the Bible is God's word and the sword of the Spirit, but a sword never drawn is useless and a Bible sitting on the bedside table is of no use unless read and applied. We all know we are to pray without ceasing, but how much time do we really spend in prayer? We all pray, "Forgive us our debts, as we forgive our debtors," but do we manifest this in reality when we are deeply offended? These are the kind of things I believe the Apostle means when he says, "Work out your own salvation."

But why with "fear and trembling"? This does not mean with fear and trembling lest we lose our salvation, for this is impossible. This is simply a way of saying this is serious business. Much is at stake – our witness in the world, our personal assurance and, above all, the glory of Christ and the blessing of a sweet and close fellowship with Him. Should we not fear and tremble if these things are threatened?

III. THE PASTORAL ENCOURAGEMENT

Now comes the most encouraging and comforting words in this entire text: "For it is God who is working in you, both to will and to do for His good pleasure."

"Praise God from whom all blessings flow!" We hear God saying through His Word, "Work out your own salvation with fear and trembling," so we fear and tremble only because we have to confess to ourselves, "But Lord, it is not in me either to will or to do your will." If God was not working in you in this way, we could not even begin to work out our salvation. Jesus understood that very well when He was talking to His disciples on the way to Gethsemane. He said, "As the branch cannot bear fruit of itself except it abides in the vine, neither can you unless you abide in Me." When my wife made her delicious pastries and bread, she had to put yeast into the dough and then knead that yeast into every part of the dough in order to make the bread rise and be ready to bake, serve, and eat. (My only contribution to this complicated process was the latter.)

I love what our Confession of Faith has to say about this under the chapter heading, "Concerning Good Works." By the way, our Confession was never intended to be a remote reference book to be placed on the shelf and maybe on rare occasion to be used to check someone's theology. The Westminster Divines who labored so carefully and diligently over the Confession and catechisms were, for the most part, active pastors and elders who served congregations and continued to preach and teach God's Word. I find them invaluable in preparing sermons and lessons, and am immeasurably helped by the simple wisdom stated in our doctrinal standards.

But now in referring to good works or, in other words, working out our salvation in fear and trembling, and in these words, "For it is God who works in you to will and to do of His good pleasure," the Confession has this to say. Believers get the ability to do good works entirely from the Spirit of Christ. In addition to the other particular effects of God's grace already received, believers must be directed by the Holy Spirit in order to will and do what pleases God. However, they are not therefore to grow spiritually lazy waiting for some special guidance from the Spirit before doing anything commanded by God. Rather, they should diligently attempt to identify the good works God has commanded in His Word, and try their best to do all of them, praying earnestly and daily for the empowering and enabling of the Holy Spirit who lives in them.

So, here you see the balance and between "work out you own salvation" and "it is God who works in you to will and do of His good pleasure." Truly in working out our salvation, "we are His workmanship created in Christ Jesus for good works."

The combination of these words, "both to will and to do of His good pleasure," brings us great hope and great challenge. What this is saying is that God will give us the will and the heart and the deep desire to love and honor Him. This is the fulfillment of the promises in Jeremiah and Ezekiel that in the New Covenant, of which we are a part, God will write His Word on our hearts, and then He will empower us, no matter how imperfectly, to begin the long, slow but sure process of "working out our salvation with fear and trembling, for it is God who works in us to will and to do of His good pleasure."

Questions for Discussion and Reflection

1. Discuss the instruction to "work out your own salvation with fear and trembling." What factors are key to a congregation's ability to continue its spiritual growth even in the absence of a strong and beloved leader?

2. Discuss sanctification as an active and on-going process. What does the process look like?

3. Identify practical ways in which you are working out your own salvation. Name additional ways in which you can add to your "whole armor of God."

4. There is an element critical to working out one's own salvation. What is that element?

5. Discuss the role of the Holy Spirit in our ability to do God's will, and the importance of not growing spiritually lazy.

13

ROLE MODELS
FOR BELIEVERS
Philippians 2:19-30

Everyone needs a few role models who serve as examples of what it means to love God and serve Him faithfully. I'm sure we all have some heroes and heroines we would do well to follow; people whose lives and testimonies say to us, "Follow me, as I follow Christ." I have been blessed to have a goodly number I can follow as role models without embarrassment or fear. Some of these I have known personally and have tried to follow their examples in many ways. Some are with the Lord now, and some are much younger than I am, but whose lives and lights help me through the wilderness of this world.

One of my great heroes of the Reformation was Heinrich Bullinger, pastor of the church in Zurich Switzerland for more than forty years. He was a friend and fellow worker with John Calvin, and he succeeded to the post of pastor of the Great Minster church in Zurich, following the death of young Ulrich Zwingli, the brilliant and brave leader of the Swiss Reformation who fell in the battle of Cappel which threatened the future of the Reformation in Switzerland. One of Bullinger's first acts was to befriend the widow and orphans of Zwingli and care for them like his own family following the tragic death of their husband and father. Not only these, but Protestant refugees from all over Europe and Great Britain, fleeing from persecution, made their way to Zurich, where they were taken in and cared for by this godly pastor and his equally godly and sacrificing wife.

Bullinger lived to a very old age, and up until the last few months of his life, he served as pastor and leader of the Swiss Reformation. The last ten years of his life, he endured great sickness and sorrows. The pestilence of 1564-5 brought him to the verge of the grave, and took his beloved wife, three of his daughters, and a beloved son-in-law. In this same era, he also lost his dearest friends and fellow workers for the Reformation: William Farel, John Calvin, and a large number of other close colleagues in the ministry. He preached his last sermon on Pentecost Sunday in 1575.

Particularly touching are some of the letters which he wrote to those who were facing martyrdom for the faith. Among these was Bishop William Hooper, who was burned at the stake in the cause of the Reformation. Lady Jane Grey found great comfort and help in her correspondence with Pastor Bullinger before being beheaded by Henry VIII. Later, Queen Elizabeth was deeply affected by the works of Bullinger, and under his influence refused to be called the head of the Church of England, saying that honor was Christ's alone.

I had the great privilege years ago of going on a Reformation tour with a group of friends from First Presbyterian Church in Macon, Georgia. One of our stops was the historic city of Zurich, and of course the church where Bullinger preached for all those many years.

It was an awe-inspiring experience to stand under the pulpit from which that hero of mine preached God's Word. When one member of our tour asked me to stand up in the pulpit to have my picture made, I could not bring myself to do this, but only to stand under the pulpit. Who was I to presume to step into the pulpit of that great prince of the Church?

Role models are a vital part of our growing in Christ. That's why God provides them for us. Here in this passage of Scripture, we have reference to two all-time great role models for believers young and old, man and woman. Their names? Timothy and Epaphroditus, friends and fellow workers with the apostle Paul in the first century, and shining lights for Jesus Christ for any century and for any believer.

I. TIMOTHY, PAUL'S SOUL BROTHER

Timothy was an early convert under the influence of his godly mother, Eunice, and grandmother, Lois, and of course the preaching and teaching of Paul. He became one of the best leaders of the Church in the first century, and the recipient of two letters from Paul which became a part of God's completed written revelation. He is mentioned over and over again in various letters the Apostle wrote, and always in a favorable light. Here in this passage, his name comes up again and with high praise and having the complete confidence of Paul. Apparently, Timothy had gone to Rome to be near Paul during his incarceration there. Paul was given a large measure of freedom and visitors were permitted to minister to his needs. What better man than Timothy, a spiritual son of Paul and dear to him as a true son. At the same time, if Paul was found guilty and was condemned, those who had been closely associated with him were also in jeopardy. So, among his many attributes were loyalty and courage.

Paul had a goodly number of friends and fellow workers: Luke, Silas, Titus, to name but a few, but of Timothy he said, "I have no one like-minded." They served the same Lord as dear brothers, or more as a father and son. He commended Timothy's sincerity in caring for the spiritual well-being of the believers in Philippi, and for always putting others ahead of himself and always putting Christ ahead of all. He was a faithful servant of Christ and of Paul. What a powerful truth is found here. One mark of a servant spirit for Christ is how we demonstrate this in our relationship to each other. Timothy had proven this by his sacrificial and never-ceasing care for Paul and for the churches he had helped Paul establish. Timothy took seriously the words of the Lord Jesus, "He who would be great among you let him be servant of all." How I wish we understood that half as well as Timothy did.

So, Timothy was chosen to represent Paul and bring encouragement and help to the saints in Philippi. Paul did not know if the news Timothy would bring to the Church would be the good news that he had been acquitted and released, or an announcement of his condemnation and death. But in either case, Timothy was chosen because he had been as a son to Paul.

Now, let me tell you something simply awesome. Christ has chosen you as his messenger and to be an encouragement to the people He loves and for whom He died. That among other things is the calling of every believer. It was Paul who said in another place, "Now we are ambassadors for Christ, as though God were pleading through us. We implore you on Christ's behalf, be reconciled to God."

II. EPAPHRODITUS: A BROTHER, FELLOW WORKER, SOLDIER, MESSENGER, & MINISTER

Now as for this man, who was not nearly so well known as Timothy, but who was equally beloved by Paul, it seems the Apostle almost ran out of superlatives in describing him. The brief facts we know about him are as follows. He was a spiritual leader in the Philippian church. The congregation there chose him to take their love gift to Paul while he was in prison, and to remain with him as a servant and helper. While engaged in this service ministry, he became very ill, almost to the point of death. The word came back to Philippi that he was ill and not expected to live, much to the distress of believers there. Many prayers were offered up for him and God graciously spared his life, much to their joy and Paul's. He was sent back home to assure the congregation of his recovery, and bring a report from the Apostle.

Paul spoke of this in verses 25-30. "I found it necessary to send back to you Epaphroditus." Now note how he was described: "My brother and fellow worker, my fellow soldier and your messenger and minister to my need." Such was Epaphroditus, whose name means "lovely." Truly, he was a man whose heart was overflowing with love, a love which expressed itself more in actions than words. Brother, worker, warrior. These words go together and are an apt description of all believers, or should be. I find them both challenging and convicting. The word 'brother' (or 'sister') reminds us that by grace we are members of one family, with one Father, and one Elder Brother who brought us before the Father for adoption. The Kingdom of God requires workers, servants who will serve at whatever cost, not only serving the Lord but serving the family members in need. Wasn't this the message Jesus gave us when He washed the disciples' feet? The word 'warrior' reminds us that the Christian family is also the

Christian army, and we are a band of brothers in the fight. Two other words which are closely tied together, or should be, are the words 'messenger' and 'minister'. Sadly, we see many cases in which the messenger is less of a minister than he ought to be, and always to the hurt of a congregation. As these words are used here, Epaphroditus was the embodiment of the congregation in Philippi. It was obvious not all of them could go to Rome to be with Paul and minister to him, but when this good man went, he went as a representative of all the body to bring Paul the love gift and minister to his needs, spiritually and materially.

We really ought to understand that in a very real sense, we, too, are the embodiment of the Church and are seen as such by the watching world. The impression you make on your neighbors and fellow workers in business is their impression not only of your home church, but of the whole Body of Christ, and yes, of Christ Himself.

Another thing about Epaphroditus was his tender heart and sensitivity to the feelings of his fellow believers. "He was longing for you all, and he was distressed because you heard he was sick." This expresses a tender heart, like the heart of Jesus. Remember when at the last supper Jesus said to His disciples, "With great desire I have desired to eat this feast with you, before I suffer." The implication was that He knew they would be comforted later by what happened at the last supper, though He Himself suffered so much.

How easily we forget that our hearts should always be open and tender towards our fellow believers. "We share our mutual woes, our mutual burdens bear, and often for each other flows, the sympathizing tear." Have you ever known a friend who wept simply because you wept, and rejoiced because you were happy? We weep for ourselves far more often than we weep for each other, but Epaphroditus, one of our role models as seen in this text, was filled with anxiety because of the anxiety of his friends back home in the church.

Mere toleration of each other is not what Jesus had in mind when He commanded us to love one another, but rather a love that expresses itself both in emotion and in loving ministry to each other. It seems when Epaphroditus thought he was on his death bed, his greatest concern was for the feelings and fears of those back home in his church. What a lovely man was this true role model.

What comes through about both of these men was the effect their lives had on others. They were the cause of praise and thanksgiving, love and appreciation by those who knew and served with them. There was the atmosphere of heaven surrounding them, and in the lives of these role models we catch a glimpse at least of what heaven will be like. Do you suppose we leave the same impression on others?

Questions for Discussion and Reflection

1. Read Philippians 2:19-30 again. What qualities do Timothy and
    Epaphroditus share?   How do these qualities set them apart from
    others with whom Paul has worked?

2. Have you ever shared in a relationship like that of Paul and
    Timothy? If so, discuss some aspects of the experience. How did
    it strengthen you spiritually? How did it strengthen you in your
    work together?

3. Have you ever had a Timothy or Epaphroditus in your life? If so,
    what did you learn from them about true servanthood?

4. Paul describes Epaphroditus as a fellow soldier. What
    characteristics does this description bring to mind? How might
    these characteristics be applied both to your personal faith life and
    to your role as a member of a community of believers?

5. Discuss the impact of a congregation's work as brother/sister,
    servant, and soldier beyond the walls of the church. What is the
    connection between serving our brethren in the faith and serving
    the mission of Jesus?

6. Using this passage as reference, what does it mean to truly love
    one another?

14

LOOKING BACK
BUT PRESSING ON
Philippians 3:1-14

Most people have an unseen letter on the doorpost of their lives.

People are driven by ambitions. Some are worthy and noble, others are less so. People are sometimes ruined by ambitions of the wrong kind and bring sorrow and suffering upon others. This may be politicians or pastors, coaches or CEOs. Throughout history there are tales of suffering and horror people have endured because of the all-consuming ambitions of godless leaders. But some people become great benefactors of mankind by unselfish and noble ambitions. Contrast the ambition of Hitler and Churchill.

I have been looking back so that I might see more clearly where I am going, but a review or study of the past alone is not a sufficient guide for the future. As a body of believers in Jesus Christ who are committed to the proposition that the inspired, inerrant Word of God is the only infallible rule of faith and practice, we know that our one true guide for the present we can see, and for the unforeseeable future, must be the Holy Scriptures. Does the Bible offer guidance in this quest to be a true servant and a true church of our Lord and Savior in the days which lie ahead? Most surely, and we must carefully seek that guidance in all we are and all we set out to do.

This passage from Philippians is the blueprint God provides for our consideration both of the past and the future, as well as the present. Of all the great and challenging words ever spoken or written by God's servant Paul, these Holy Spirit-inspired words stand as a guiding light as we contemplate the future God has for us. "... One thing I do: forgetting what lies behind, and reaching forward to what lies ahead, I press on towards the goal for the prize of the upward call of God in Christ Jesus." Let's consider this word from God in the context in which it was written, and discover what this means for the Church as it serves the Lord, and for you personally while waiting for His return.

I. PAUL'S PAST

A. His Pre-Christian Days as Saul

Before He was found of Christ on the Damascus road, Saul had a pure lineage and impeccable credentials as the quintessential Jew. He was born of pure Hebrew stock of the tribe of Benjamin. He called himself a "Hebrew of the Hebrews," an idiomatic expression to say, in effect, the purest of the pure: a Hebrew son of Hebrew parents.

Moreover, they had claimed him as an heir of the covenant God made with Abraham. That was not all. He had been brought up in a strict Jewish family, taught the Word of God, and the sacred history of God's chosen people. In fact, he had surpassed his fellow students and had been permitted to study under one of the greatest scholars of the Jews, Gamaliel. He had united himself to the party of the Pharisees, the heroic defenders of the Jewish state and the Jewish religion. His Father had gained Roman citizenship by some outstanding deed of service to the Roman Empire, and Saul had inherited that privilege.

When the sect of the Nazarine, whom some called Christians, began to spread and threaten the old ways, Saul became the most zealous persecutor of those who would bring trouble upon Israel. He took an active and leading role in the effort to exterminate this heresy, and to bring its followers to prison and to death. As a good Jew, he was blameless!

It was in the process of this attempt to persecute to extinction this terrible threat, He was found by Christ. You know the story all too well to have need of me to recount that remarkable conversion from chief antagonist to chief protagonist, but when it happened, a radical change in attitude and actions took place immediately. All of those things in which he gloried and took such pride suddenly meant nothing! The wonder and glory of knowing Jesus Christ as the Messiah and his own Lord and Savior was so great, he discarded all his former accolades and achievements as if they were only rubbish to be thrown away. His ambition was radically altered!

B. His Post-conversion Experiences as a Christian

He experienced one of the most dramatic conversions ever recorded. He was shown visions of glory no earth-bound man had ever seen. He was the leading apologist for Christianity. He was a great scholar and profound theologian. He was an incredible evangelist, and the pioneer missionary with a vision of a world won to Christ. This, too, was a part of Paul's past when he wrote these words.

II. THE AMAZING TRANSFORMATION OF VALUES

Isn't it amazing how a genuine experience with Christ changes our outlook and our sense of what is really important? Paul had been captured by higher and nobler ambitions on the Damascus road. First, his desire was to be "found in Christ." This speaks of a right position or status – namely, justification – that comes by grace through faith. But that was not enough. He also wanted a very deep personal relationship with the Lord Jesus. He said, "That I may know Him, and the power of his resurrection, and the fellowship of His suffering, being conformed to His death." These things had become the meaning and the passion of his life. In a very real sense, this is the definition of what it means to be a Christian. I wish more of us understood how absolutely essential this transformation of values is to validate our claim to belong to Christ.

III. PAUL'S PRESENT DETERMINATION AND FUTURE HOPE

"This one thing I do ..." He now is a man with a glorious past, at least from the world's point of view, and a commendable record as a Christian, but his present determination compels him to press on. "This one thing ..." I love those words. They speak of a person whose life is gloriously focused. This man took to heart the words of Christ, "blessed are the pure in heart." The absence of this compelling drive leaves most Christians weak, confused, and ineffective. Jesus said to the rich young ruler, "One thing you lack ..." Mary, the sister of Martha, understood the one thing in life which was more important than anything else. The Psalmist of old wrote, "One thing have I desired of the Lord, that will I seek after."

Now Paul had discovered one thing worth dying for, which made life worth living. Similarly, many democratic countries, including America, fight terrorists in far away lands. Many have discovered the same thing discovered in World War II, Korea, and Viet Nam. Freedom is worth dying for. That makes "life, liberty, and the pursuit of happiness" more cherished than ever before. You see it each day as a gift from God, and you are determined to make your life count for Him. We have been greatly blessed beyond our own understanding by the lives of those who have served and fought for our freedom.

So, Paul said, "This one thing I do, forgetting what lies behind ..." What did he mean by those words, and how would that apply to us? First, what it doesn't mean is to blank out all the past, or pretend it had never happened. He could still remember his days as an unbeliever. He would always remember that wondrous day when Christ met him on the Damascus road. He often recounted his past as a traveling missionary; the good times and the trying times as well. What he meant was that he would never be content with his present progress. He wanted a deeper and dearer walk with the Lord. He knew that yesterday's accomplishments would not suffice for tomorrow. How ridiculous it would be for an Olympic athlete to run three of four laps, and then stop, look back, and gloat over being in the lead for part of the race. Even more foolish for believers or congregations to look back and revel in the past and rest contented with where they are and the accomplishments of the past.

So, putting the past behind him, Paul fixed his eyes and his ambitions on the future with these words, repeated twice, "I press on." This expression graphically pictures the marathon runner who has endured and persevered and now in the distance sees the goal for which he has been running; the goal for which he has been training for many long months. With eagerness and whole-hearted determination, he sees nothing but that goal and all energy of mind, body, and spirit are focused on that glorious destiny. To lose when so near the goal would be tragic, so he presses on. But it's not just the pillar that marks the goal; it is the prize that lies beyond the goal. For the ancient runner, it was a crown of fading laurel leaves; for Paul, the crown of life which would never perish. For the runner, it meant praise and honors from his city; for Paul, it meant hearing his Lord say, "Well done, good and faithful servant." And even more, it meant his life-long ambition would at last be fulfilled; he would be conformed to the image of Christ.

What is your highest ambition? Let me sincerely suggest that there is only one ambition worthy to claim that first place in your life. This ambition alone can transform all lesser ambitions into a part of that holy pursuit. Yes, be the best husband or father or wife or mother you can possibly be. Be the best farmer, the best doctor, the best teacher, the best lawyer, the best athlete, or the best whatever you long to be. But this one thing above all else I challenge you to be: Be the most Christ-like, the best Christian you can possibly be, that you may know Him fully and be like Him truly. If that is your highest goal, you will succeed, for He promised, "Blessed are they who hunger and thirst after righteousness, for they shall be filled."

Questions for Discussion and Reflection

1. What does it mean to be "found in Christ"?

2. Can you point to a genuine transforming event in your personal life that led to a conversion in your faith life? Discuss or journal about the event and how it transformed your heart and mind.

3. What is the value to the Christian life in "forgetting what lies behind and straining forward"?

4. Paul's highest ambition was to hear his Lord say, "Well done, good and faithful servant." What is your highest ambition?

15

AN INSIGHTFUL AUTOBIOGRAPHY

Philippians 3:4-16

I wish you could have known one of my favorite seminary professors, and I wish I had known him longer and better. Dr. J. B. Green was a remarkable man in many ways. He was an intelligent and even brilliant scholar. He was a good theologian, a remarkable biblical exegete, a captivating preacher, and a compelling lecturer. He was one of the few men I have ever heard who was able to communicate more truth in a simpler way than most who strive for eloquence and speak in complicated sentences in order to impress people with their great learning. He was also one of the few speakers who used subtle humor effectively without being carried away with his own sense of performance. When asked in class one day how soon a young man should marry, his response was classic: "As soon as possible and as often as necessary." (He himself had outlived two wives and had recently taken on another one, which in the minds of some would cause them to question his wisdom and maybe even his sanity).

He had been retired for several years when I was in seminary, but he came back on occasion to teach elective courses at the eager request of the faculty and student body. I was privileged to study the book of Philippians under him. In fact, so far as I know, this was the last seminary class he ever taught. What Dr. Green gave me was a lasting appreciation of this book, at least a degree of understanding of its message, and an excellent sermon outline of this third chapter which I now pass on to you. It is quite simple, but at the same time very profound. One of the frustrating things about his lectures was that he made us fill in the blanks and think for ourselves so far as application is concerned, and I thank him for this.

I don't remember that he called this Paul's autobiography, or even a road map of his spiritual journey, but it was both. The first point was: WHAT SAUL THOUGHT OF SAUL. The second point was: WHAT PAUL THOUGHT OF SAUL. The third point was: WHAT PAUL THOUGHT OF PAUL. I've never found a better outline on these verses and on the theme of them than this. The brilliant outline is Dr. Green's. The blundering attempt to fill in the blanks is all mine.

I. SAUL'S OPINION OF SAUL

As this third chapter develops, we hear the Apostle reflecting on his former life before Christ met him and called him on the Damascus road. Let me tell you first of all, Paul was not doing what some believers do when called upon to give their testimony. I have heard men give a long testimony and spend the majority of the time talking about their past life, almost as if they were proud of their sinful record. What Paul was doing was refuting the arguments of the Judaizers who seemed to place greater value on their Jewish credentials, such as the mere formality of submitting to physical circumcision as a guarantee of salvation, rather than on their relationship to Jesus Christ. His point is to say that his Jewish credentials could match and exceed theirs, but they were of no value to him as a follower of Christ.

So, he used their own arguments against them. "If anyone thinks he may have confidence in the flesh, I more so" was the way he put it. He was an authentic Jew! He received the sign of covenantal cleansing, but he was not thereby inwardly clean. He was circumcised on the eighth day according to the Law of Moses. He was a direct descendent of Abraham, Isaac, and Jacob – a member of the chosen race. He was even from the tribe of Benjamin. Why this was a special honor for Jews may only be surmised, but perhaps it was because Benjamin was the only son of Jacob who was born in the Promised Land. He called himself, "A Hebrew of the Hebrews", which was an idiom to express the unquestionable purity of his lineage.

Then, beyond heritage were his achievements. He was a Pharisee of the strictest sect. Yes, the Pharisees had fallen far from their original purpose, but still many of them were of noble character and noted achievement. They were patriots and defenders of the faith and of the Jewish culture as opposed to the corrupting influence of the Sadducees, who were hopelessly compromised with the Greco-Roman culture. They were the conservatives who resisted the humanistic influences of the Greeks. Being a Pharisee, he had kept the law as interpreted by the scribes and lawyers ... the lengthy commentaries which had accumulated over hundreds of years, known as the Mishnah. They thought if they kept the law as they understood it, the Messiah would come as a result of their efforts. But when the Messiah did come, He revealed how far they had strayed away from the true law of God, and how they had violated the spirit of the law by their excessive demands which had little relationship to God's law. They naturally became very self-righteous and exceedingly proud of their supposed learning, looking down on the rest of the human race, even Jews, as "rabble that did not know the law." Some, a few, saw through the insufficiency of all this, and one of the better ones, Nicodemus, came to Jesus hoping to find some new truth or some new way of understanding God's law.

Apparently, Saul was considered by many to be THE rising star of this whole sect. Were the Judaizers of Philippi zealous in their efforts to make the Church more Jewish? Saul could match their zeal. They might rail against the Gentile converts, Saul did better. He persecuted the Church, having some cast into prison for torture, others to be killed. As Dr. William Hendiksen observed in his commentary, "If persecuting zeal could ever open the gates of heaven, Saul would have walked right in." So, this man could claim to be blameless in his outward faithfulness to what the Mishnah said the law of God meant. Could these first century Judaizers say the same? Can we? Now we move on to:

II. PAUL'S OPINION OF SAUL

As Saul, he had been so proud of his birthright and his remarkable achievements. But that was before the meeting with the risen Christ on the road to Damascus, and the hard years of re-studying the Scriptures he thought he had known so well. Listen to how he looked at his former glory after coming to Christ. "But what things were gain to me, these I have counted loss for Christ. Yes indeed, I also count all things loss for the excellence of the knowledge of Christ Jesus, my Lord, for Whom I have suffered the loss of all things and count them as rubbish."

No doubt the futility of his efforts must have nagged at Saul, and especially comparing his spirit with that of the martyr Stephen, whom he helped to kill. That man had died in great peace, and in victory, even forgiving his tormentors. But that only prepared Saul for what was truly the great life-changing event of his life. Christ, whose Church he was attempting to destroy, revealed Himself in a blaze of glorious, blinding light, and called him by name, and by sin, and then by a grace so wonderful that he finally saw himself for what he was: a self-deluded, hell-bound sinner whose righteousness was nothing more than an illusion and a sham. Instantly, all those things he had counted so precious became vile, and all those things he had looked upon as vile, namely faith in Jesus as the Messiah, became precious, the pearl of great price, for which he would sell all – nay, abandon all –that he might have that pearl, that righteousness which comes by faith alone and by no human effort.

Not that the many things for which he was once proud were bad in and of themselves, but they had been barriers to faith and had produced pride, self-righteousness, and a haughty spirit towards others. One may well be willing to surrender a vice for Christ's sake, but to surrender what one had always thought a great virtue is quite another. That is when the heart is truly broken before God, and that is exactly when the gift of eternal life through Jesus Christ may be received and by which we may become truly righteous, but no longer self-righteous.

It is of great profit to know that after thirty years of serving, suffering for Jesus' sake, he still considered all personal achievements of his self-righteous past to be nothing more than rubbish, and dangerous rubbish at that. He used the ongoing tense when he said "I still count all things in which I once gloried as pure rubbish compared to the excellence of the knowledge of Christ."

III. PAUL'S OPINION OF PAUL

A. By way of a truly holy ambition

As Saul, he had set out to prove he was the most righteous man in the world, only to discover he was the chief of sinners. But now, as Paul, born again from above, he had turned only to Christ and a holy desire to be found in Him, not having a righteousness of his own achievement but the righteousness which is granted us by grace through faith. And that righteousness is perfect, complete, and forever. And by that righteousness, we may truly know Him and the power of His resurrection, the fellowship of His suffering, being conformed to His death, that we may attain to the resurrection of the dead. That is the goal of every believer. But what about the present experience, even of such a giant as Paul?

B. By way of present experience

"Not that I have already attained, or am already perfected, but I press on that I may lay hold of that for which Christ also laid hold of me. Brethren, I do not count myself to have laid hold, but this one thing I do: forgetting those things which are behind, reaching forward to those things which are ahead, I press on towards the goal." Summary: "I'm not there yet, but I am forgetting what is behind me, both the bad, and the good, keeping my heart on what lies ahead, fellowship with Christ now and later in heaven, I keep going on." No wonder the devil hated Paul so much. He never gave up, even though hurt and discouraged by the failure of others and himself. He kept looking to Jesus, trusting in Jesus, longing to see Jesus one day; and because this was his true heart's desire, and because he would keep his eyes on that glorious goal, he made it one day, and following the same path, so will I, and so will you.

Questions for Discussion and Reflection

1. Why was Saul's pre-Christian life a source of pride to him

2. Saul was a very religious person before meeting Christ on the road to Damascus. What is the difference between being religious and knowing Christ?

3. Why was Paul willing to give up his "Saul life" for Christ?

4. What was Paul's true heart's desire? What is yours?

16

HEAVENLY CITIZENSHIP
Philippians 3:12-21

If you have ever wondered how and why the Apostle could drive himself unceasingly in the ministry, endure almost unbelievable hardship and danger, never flinch in the face of opposition, cruel torture, and face certain death so calmly and even joyfully, you have to look no further than these verses. I think to get the full impact of the climactic verses 20 and 21, we have to go back to those words of Paul about pressing on as seen in verses 12-14.

When he said, "not that I have already attained or am already perfected, but I press on that I may lay hold of that for which Christ Jesus has also laid hold of me," he was expanding the meaning of salvation to its deepest meaning and farthermost extent. In that sense, he was saying, "My salvation is not yet complete." Now, that thought shocks people who only see salvation as mere justification, somehow disconnected from sanctification and glorification. While it is true we are justified by faith alone apart from the works of the law, it is also true that the faith which justifies is never alone. That is to say, the new birth is demonstrated by the new life in Christ. So, we walk a careful razor's edge in our definitions, which is precisely what we must do lest we err greatly by straying off the clear teaching of Scripture by excess emphasis on one aspect of truth at the expense of others.

Surely, if the apostle Paul had to admit he had not yet attained, had not yet been perfected, had not yet even apprehended, then all the false notions of perfectionism by whatever name must be laid aside. But notice the splendid balance. He knew some day in glory he would be made perfect in holiness, and he also knew since this was true, his goal, though presently unattainable, even in this life must be nothing less, nor should our goal be anything less. So he laid aside the past, pressed on towards that goal with dogged perseverance, always reaching out for that which would always be beyond his reach in this life, but assured the goal would be reached at last. He referred to this as "the goal of the upward call of God in Christ Jesus."

Then in verses 15-16, we hear him exhort, "Therefore, let us, as many as are mature have this mind." There is a vast difference between perfection and maturity, though sometimes in Scripture the meaning of 'perfect' is 'maturity' as opposed to complete sinlessness. I think one of the marks of a mature believer is the recognition of the ongoing problem of sin which needs constantly to be confessed, and by God's grace accepting the promises of forgiveness and cleansing. But I think the point Paul is making is that another measure of our maturity in the faith is to recognize what he has said both about acknowledging our imperfections, and at the same time pressing on towards the goal of laying hold of that for which Christ has laid hold of us. He also invites us to make sure our lives match our profession, which is also another part of our ongoing struggle. He put it this way, "To the degree to which you have already attained, let us walk by the same rule."

The very serious warning contained in verses 17-19 cannot be ignored. He begins by inviting believers to follow his example. Was this proud boasting? Not at all, for even knowing his imperfections he still lived an exemplary life. But the emphasis here is still the "pressing on" and not being satisfied with our present attainments in obedience. So he was not saying, "Follow me because I am perfect," but "Follow me in my zeal for striving after holiness of life."

It seems a bit ironic that Paul begins this chapter warning against the legalists, and now has to deal with the hedonists who live and teach a perverted doctrine of grace. It is true that we must walk that thin line because human nature tends to run towards the excess in whatever direction it chooses to follow. I heard a man once say, "Psychology precedes theology." Later, when I asked him what he meant, he explained it something like this. "The same kind of people I knew as a boy who were adamantly Dispensational in their theology are very much like the people I know now who are adamantly Reformed. The key word is adamant." Although I didn't totally agree with him, I saw what he meant and had observed the same tendencies in folks I have known. There is an old saying, "A cowboy lives off the fat of the land." There is another old saying I just made up, "The modern Christian lives off the fad of the times." But back to the verses here. The legalist has no joy, replacing it with self-righteousness. The hedonist thinks pleasure is joy and knows little of true joy. One of the woeful side effects of either extreme is that a very perverted idea of Christianity is presented to unbelievers. So, the hedonist, who lives only for the fleeting pleasures of this world as opposed to the eternal joys of heaven, is just as much an enemy of the cross as the legalist who seeks self-justification on the basis of works.

I hope you will notice something else at this point about the spirit of the Apostle in dealing with those who were perverting the Gospel by their worldly living: "I have told you often and now tell you even weeping that they are the enemies of the cross of Christ..." Oh, if only we had that same heartbroken attitude towards those who are of that same persuasion, sorrow from the depths of our being towards such people who are missing out on the Kingdom. Let me tell you a story which speaks to the point I am trying to make. A certain church up in the mountains of Tennessee was seeking a pastor. So, they elected a search committee to seek out a man for the position. (What would churches do if they didn't have committees?) They worked long and hard seeking a pastor who would fit their congregation. At last, the committee narrowed their choice down to two men. So, they arranged for visits on successive Sundays to each church. The pastor on that first Sunday preached on the text, "The wicked shall be cast into Hell." It was a powerful sermon, well developed, and biblical. After the service, the committee met to discuss what they had heard and their reaction to the pastor. Their opinions were generally favorable. The committee's chairman was quiet, which was unusual for him, and he made no comment. "What do you think Mr. Chairman," asked one of the younger members on the committee. "I think it would be a dreadful mistake to recommend that man as pastor of our church. Let's hear what the other pastor preaches on and what we think of his sermon." So, they agreed to the suggestion and met at the other church the next Sunday. As God would have it, the next pastor preached on the same text that the first one preached from. At the committee meeting following that service the young man who had sought the chairman's opinion the week before offered the opinion, "that since the chairman has already expressed his opposition to the sermon and the pastor last Sunday, we know what his recommendation will be about this pastor, but we'll ask him just to make sure." The chairman's response surprised them all. "I think," he said, "he's just the man we need and furthermore, I think we ought to take a vote to call him as our pastor." The other committee members were very surprised at his words. "But why would you vote for this man? He said virtually the same things we heard the other pastor say?" "So he did," the chairman said, "but this man said them with a broken heart and tears in his eyes from the very start." (From what I heard, the church grew and prospered and brought many who were destined for hell into the Kingdom."

The more we follow the example of Paul in this attitude, the more effective our witness will be.

In practically every epistle of the New Testament, all of which were written to professing Christians, there are serious warnings about ungodly living and constant calls for repentance from the sins of the world, the flesh, and the devil into which believers had fallen. It is obvious that first century Christians were dealing with some of the same pressures to which we are constantly exposed. The culture had become corrupted not only by the excesses of wealth, but also by the pagan influences of Greco-Roman philosophy, the strange sects which proliferated in the early Church – some of which encouraged and promoted immorality in the name of freedom – and even within more orthodox circles. Even the Church had been so corrupted that the doctrine of grace had been used to allow and justify almost any conduct. In short, the Church then faced what we face now – namely, being conformed to this world rather than being transformed by God's Word.

Now we move to the heart of this part of Scripture. In verses 20-21, the Apostle sums up the whole meaning and goal of his life, and explains the urgency of what he has been writing. "For," he said, "Our homeland is in heaven." Listen to this brilliant but brief commentary by Dr. William Hendriksen on those words: "...These Christians living in Philippi must realize that their homeland ... has fixed its location in heaven. It was heaven that gave them birth, for they are born from above. Their names are inscribed on heaven's register. Their lives are governed from heaven, and in accordance with heaven's standards. Their rights are secured in heaven. Their interests are being promoted there. To heaven their thoughts and prayers ascend, and their hopes aspire. Many of their friends (and loved ones) and members of their fellowship are there now, and they themselves, the citizens of the heavenly kingdom still on earth, will shortly follow. In heaven their inheritance awaits them. Their heavenly mansions are being prepared ... on earth they are strangers, sojourners, and pilgrims. 'They desire a better country, that is a heavenly one. Therefore God is not ashamed to be called their God, for he has prepared for them a city.'"

Paul then adds, "But our citizenship is in heaven, and from it we await a Savior, the Lord Jesus Christ." The expectation of Christ's return is a powerful motivation for the pursuit of holiness and following the pattern of behavior set down in these previous verses. Our present life is rehearsal, but what gives it meaning is the concert for which we are rehearsing. I am reminded of a choir in one of the congregations I served. It was the best choir and the finest music this side of heaven, but the music didn't "just happen." The choir would rehearse over and over again. The greater the music, the harder they worked. One example of this was an Easter celebration. All of the music was lovely and most of it was difficult to sing. So, the choir spent untold hours rehearsing, and after each rehearsal the music director spent untold sleepless hours. Then came Easter evening, and what we heard that night presented the message of Easter in all its beauty and power. Had that event not occurred, the long hours in rehearsal would have been pointless and even pathetic. So, in a very real sense, we are rehearsing for heaven. Most of us fumble and stumble along, we hit the wrong notes, and often are off key, but still we persevere, or rather God perseveres in us. Then one day, the rehearsal will be completed and the real music will begin. The analogy is far from perfect but it's the best I can do.

There is one word I don't want you to overlook, and that is "eagerly." We eagerly await our Savior, the Lord Jesus Christ. Yes, I know He is coming to judge, but our Judge is also our Savior, who alone can vindicate us by His blood and righteousness. And He will recreate our lowly bodies that they may conform to His glorious body.

I served a very small church in Atlanta, Georgia many years ago. The name of the church was Wee Kirk Presbyterian. It had an interesting history behind it. The lady who gave the property and the money to build did so with certain stipulations. She was a direct descendant of the Annie Laurie of Scottish tradition, fame, and song. So, she wanted to build a church just like the Wee Kirk of the Heather. There was just one problem – that church building no longer existed. It had been built in the eleventh century but had long since had fallen into ruin and disappeared. However, the plans for the building were preserved in two places and were available to be copied. And so they were to the last detail, even including the wishing chair where young married couples sat after the wedding and wished for a happy marriage.

However, the original Wee Kirk presented certain problems for a modern church building. There was no running water (and of course no indoor plumbing.) There was no heat nor cooling and no hope of getting approval from the county to allow building such a building. Of course, these modern necessities were added to the plans to build. But according to the plans copied, the church looked just like the old Wee Kirk of the Heather and permission was granted by the county and by the modern Annie Laurie, who joyfully gave both land and money so that the modern Wee Kirk looked just like the original but with glorious and needed additions. The point is that in the New Creation, you will still be you but with the glorious additions of perfections such as sinlessness and new power to serve the Lord in a way suitable to His will. "Therefore my beloved and longed-for brethren, my joy and my crown, so stand fast in the Lord, beloved."

Questions for Discussion and Reflection

1. What does Paul mean by "the goal of the upward call of God in Christ Jesus"?

2. What is the purpose of "pressing on" in our spiritual journey?

3. What does Paul cite as a powerful motivation for the constant pursuit of holiness?

4. What are some markers of a mature faith?

5. Reflect upon the idea of your life matching your profession of faith. Discuss this idea with your study group (or friends or family). Later, set aside time to journal specifically about your life. Look at each element of the profession of faith found in either the Nicene Creed or the Apostles' Creed. How does your life, or your approach to life, illustrate each tenet of the faith?

17

CHRIST-CONTROLLED THINKING
Philippians 4

Meditation is not something we do in this busy, helter-skelter world of ours. In fact, it almost seems absurd, or at least futile, to ask people to even stop, look, and listen, let alone THINK. And yet, it is out of our "thought life" that who we are and all that we do take shape. In the epistle to the Romans, we are reminded that the way to become living sacrifices which honor the Lord is by the renewing of our minds. And as that passage develops, it is obvious the Apostle means much more than just cramming our minds full of facts and knowledge. Often in Scripture, the words 'mind' and 'heart' are used almost interchangeably. In the biblical sense, the heart means the seat of life and strength, so it means mind, soul, one's entire emotional nature, and includes also understanding. For instance, Jesus said "Out of the heart of men proceed all evil thoughts." He goes on to list some of these. The point is that He linked heart and mind as the source of evil, which is why it is so important to be constantly "renewing our minds."

Here in this passage of Scripture from Philippians, believers are exhorted to deeply think about certain things and let their minds and hearts dwell on certain ideals with the strong indication that if we will follow this formula, we will become this kind of person. Furthermore, we may actually see a model of this as we observe and consider the life of Paul, or for that matter any mature, Christ-like person. Let me tell you right away that what the Bible has in mind at this point is not at all similar to the oriental mystic New Age craze which once captured the minds of many people around the world, and especially the young adult age of perpetual college and grad school mentality so prevalent among the 'elite' in our culture.

If we reverse the order of this verse slightly, it may become clearer what the Apostle intends in this eighth verse. "You should be deeply meditating on things which are virtuous and praise-worthy such as whatever is true, noble, just, pure, lovely, and of good report."

Now let's break this down into these categories and see if we may grasp what this exhortation is all about.

I. WHATEVER THINGS ARE TRUE

In Ephesians, truth is pictured as a part of the Christian's armor as he wars against Satan. Here we are encouraged to meditate on truth as part of the inner strength which God supplies through His Word. The only way to meditate on truth is to meditate on God's Word. Jesus prayed for His disciples to the Father saying, "Sanctify them by Your truth. Your word is truth." Meditating on the Word of God includes understanding its meaning and how it applies to the issues which we face and the decisions we must make. Truth is never merely abstract or theoretical; it is always intensely practical. As we meditate on the truth God has revealed, we see more clearly not only what duty God requires in general, but more specifically what He requires and desires of us. This is a never-ending search and process. Meditating on God's Word is reading with understanding, seeking a deeper understanding and commitment to that truth, and examining and amending our lives by that truth. Nothing will serve better in making you into a truthful person than this.

II. WHATEVER THINGS ARE NOBLE

This speaks of honor and worth. It is the opposite of both base and frivolous thinking. We think nobly when we consider how we are to treat our enemies, how we are to deal with our neighbors, how we are to react to those who treat us poorly and even despitefully. It speaks of good manners, which along with meditation is a lost art in itself. It is a sad commentary on our culture to remember that when I was teaching in seminary, we had a very gracious lady who came and taught a short course on ministerial manners both in and out of the pulpit. It is even sadder to remember how sorely this was needed, and probably even more so now. In a culture which has largely lost the sense of honor and honorable things, a Christian's light will shine brightly in such a setting as we meditate on that which is honorable and put it into practice.

III. WHATEVER THINGS ARE JUST

God places a very high priority on justice. Many of His laws as seen in the books of the law in the Old Testament are laws which ensure justice, especially to the weak and oppressed. When describing righteous people such as Noah and others, the Bible refers to them as men who were upright and just. Micah summed up all that God requires of us in these words, "What does the Lord require of you,

but to do justly, love mercy, and walk humbly with your God." In
Samuel we read, "He who rules over men must be just." Why does
God emphasize justice so very much in His Word? Because He is
a just God and cares deeply about justice. It may well be said that
"in His mercy, God requires justice." As we meditate on the biblical
teaching of justice, we find ourselves being deeply convicted and
determined to always act justly in our dealings with each other.
There is nothing which will undermine a Christian's witness in
this world than to act unjustly towards others. On the other hand,
a reputation of being a just person paves the way for minds to be
opened to the truth of the Gospel.

IV. WHATEVER THINGS ARE PURE

How very, very important it is for us to dwell on what is pure. Like
the Philippians of old, we are living in a culture which laughs at and
abhors purity, and glorifies every form and expression of impurity.
I think this is tied in very closely with modesty, another forgotten
virtue; modesty of speech and action, modesty of dress and manner.
We have become so overwhelmed by the values of the world that we
accept its manner of speech, dress, and conduct without a second
thought. Even the subconscious influence of immodesty and impurity
of action, words, drama, literature, television, Internet, and daily
conversation in the work place is almost irresistible.

But there is much more implied in this word 'pure', then just purity
of thought in the realm of sexual conduct. Often times in the Bible,
you will find the word 'pure' or 'purity' in reference to sincerity. We
use the word that way, too. We speak of pure metal – that is metal
without alloy. We speak of pure orange juice, by which we mean it is
not watered down. So it is well to meditate on how to be a believer

in Christ, not watered down by the influences of the world. So as we meditate on that which is pure, we are overcoming evil with good. We are sweeping out the evil spirits and replacing them with the good and pure things which build our minds up and crowd out the impure thoughts. This is the only way, for just deciding you will refrain from evil thoughts is a losing battle unless you replace them with meditation on that which is pure in the full sense of the word.

V. WHATEVER THINGS ARE LOVELY

This word is seldom used in the Bible, and maybe even less in common speech today. By being told to meditate on that which is lovely, we are encouraged to think of those which evoke love and express love. There is a strong connection between this word and the word 'charity' in the classical sense of that word, which simply means 'unearned love'. How may we best express love to each other? How may I show love to people I don't especially like? How may I respond in love to those who speak evil of me, and show despite in their attitude and actions towards me? Many people like to plot revenge on those whom they believe have wronged them. It is so easy to feed on thoughts of anger, self-justification (even when we know we are wrong), "getting even" with one who has done or said something very hurtful to or about us. Here, we are encouraged to think in just the opposite way, and "plot" on how we may do good to those kinds of people. How revolutionary can you get?

VI. WHATEVER THINGS ARE OF GOOD REPORT

I think the best way to understand this is to think of those things which even unbelievers would applaud ... kindness, mercy, taking care of, ministering to the needs of, lending a helping hand to, and generally treating other people as they wish to be treated. A few years ago, one of the former greats of baseball lay dying. His name was Mickey Mantle. Most of you have heard of him and many remember seeing some of his exploits on the field. He was truly a gifted and amazing athlete. His career was cut short partially through injury, but mostly because of a life of dissipation and intoxication. There was another man on the same Yankee team who was the opposite of Mantle in many ways. His name was Bobby Richardson, now a retired Baptist preacher. Mickey used to make fun of Bobby because of his Christian faith and life, but secretly admired him, too. As death drew near for Mickey at the end of a wasted life, he called for Bobby to come to his death bed and talk to him about God. Bobby reports that Mickey made a sincere commitment of repentance and faith in Christ just before he died, and said as much at Mickey's funeral which he was asked to preach. Only God knows where Mickey is today, but we join Bobby in fervently hoping his last days' change was a real work of grace. But the point is that Mickey saw in Bobby what Paul called on the Philippians to see in him, and to follow his living example of one who was filled with virtue and whose life was a praise to God. The rewards of this are incredible. Not only will we have the peace of God, which is a great blessing, but even more and far better we will have Him at our side, the God of peace. And the giver is greater than the gift.

Questions for Discussion and Reflection

1. In the biblical sense, 'heart' means the seat of life and strength, so it means mind, soul, one's entire emotional nature, and also includes understanding.   Why is it important that we constantly guard or renew (vs. 7) our hearts and minds?

2. What does it mean to mediate on God's Word? Hint: What study practices must one employ to gain understanding when meditating upon the Word?

3. Review the formula laid out for us in Philippians 4:8. List each element of the formula, and then discuss a definition of each.

18

A NEEDED MINISTRY
Philippians 4:1-3

While our citizenship is in heaven, we still live on earth and deal with earthly matters. Even the best and most noble of believers are constantly in need of grace, for though we are redeemed sinners, we are still sinners. We live in a fallen world, and we live in our fallen natures and with others who are in the same boat. Moreover, some Christians are farther along in the process of sanctification than others, and some are not as far along as they should be. So within the Church, there are and always will be problems, especially, it seems, between those in positions of leadership and who are highly gifted in some areas of ministry. One cannot read the New Testament epistles and fail to notice the many references to relational problems in the early Church. And they were the same kind of problems we still have in the Body of Christ. Yes, we Christians have been baptized with the Holy Spirit, and we have been born from above, but the lower nature still plagues us. Just look at what was going on in Corinth, for instance. Paul referred to the believers there as "beloved brothers," but he found it necessary to warn and chastise them for many sins and faults. After some opening greetings, Paul then expressed great confidence and appreciation for the saints there, and even more confidence that the Lord would continue to bless them and mature them in the faith. But almost in the same breath, he also reproached them for a deeply divided party spirit within the Church. Later in the epistle, he spoke out sternly against the ethical and moral problems which were weakening the effectiveness of the Church's witness in the world. He rebuked them for failure to discipline immoral behavior of the worst sort, and later had to rebuke them for their unforgiving spirit towards a brother who had been disciplined but had repented.

As you read further through the epistles, you discover such problems as anger between believers, envy, strife, jealousy, back biting, striving for prominence and position, and all the ugly things the Church in all ages has had to confront. As the epistle to the Philippians draws towards its end, we hear the Apostle pleading with a dear brother in that congregation to lend a healing, guiding hand to two elect ladies who seemed to be having problems with each other. So, let's look at these short verses and see if we may discover some principles of Body life to guide us.

I. THE EXPRESSION & ASSURANCE OF LOVING CARE BY THE APOSTLE

Paul wisely began his appeal, both to the two women and to the one to whom he would appeal to lend a helping, reconciling hand, by assuring them all of how dear this whole body of believers had become to him. He calls them his beloved and longed-for brothers, his joy and his crown. With such expressions of appreciation and love, he could now make his appeal for unity of heart and mind. The more we know someone really cares for us, the more willing we are to listen even to words of rebuke, if they are needed. This goes much deeper than just saying something like, "I'm only saying this for your good," which may or may not be true. But since Paul had proved his love by past actions, and since these words are so obviously sincere, the hearts and ears of those to whom he will make his appeal could only be soft and pliable towards the Apostle.

First, there is a general appeal to the whole body of believers to stand fast in the Lord. No doubt the church had been through much suffering, as we are reminded earlier in this same epistle. The world around them was both hostile and at the same time alluring them to return to the old ways of living they had known before they met the Lord. The many sub-Christian sects that had proliferated in that day and ours, were attempting to draw them away from the truth revealed in God's Word to be replaced by human wisdom, so-called. In their own ranks, the legalists and the libertines were vying for controlling influence in the congregation. "Stand fast" was a very timely word, as it always is for believers. The following appeal to two apparently very strong-willed individuals was set in this context. So, the Apostle well knew that dissension within the ranks of the true believers would lessen their influence and weaken their ability to resist all these ungodly pressures which threatened the Church. Do we understand that? Unless there is a deep-seated spirit of unity within the body, even when there are strong differences of opinion, there is little chance many will hear and respond to our proclamation and teaching of the truth. Sometimes, we are tempted to think and act as if we think, "so long as I am standing firm on my understanding of the truth, it makes little difference how I stand for that truth." I was talking with a ruling elder in another congregation in another state about how things were progressing in that congregation. I had been privileged to lend them a helping hand years ago in a time of controversy. He was commenting on their former pastor's way of dealing with people. He was and is well known for his zeal for truth and for his unquestioned orthodoxy in theology, which is always commendable. But this elder's comment on that pastor was something like this: "Those of us on the Session spent most of our time following the pastor around, and either picking up dead bodies in his train or else the badly wounded and barely alive church members whom he had trampled on in his zeal for truth; a sad commentary indeed. It doesn't have to be that way. It is not either-or. Paul knew that the unity of the body was being threatened, and the witness of the body dimmed by feuding church members.

II. HIS APPEAL TO THE TWO LADIES INVOLVED

Notice how skillful and even-handed he is in addressing these elect ladies. He did not say, "I implore Euodia and Syntyche to be of one mind." He said, "I implore Euodia, and I implore Syntyche." So, this was a personal appeal to each one of them, no matter how the other might respond. By this, he is expressing equal esteem for each of them, and holding each responsible for their reaction to this appeal.

What more do we know or may logically infer from this situation? Well, first of all, they were members of the congregation in Philippi and probably had been for some time, and probably from the very beginning. They had been "fellow workers" with the Apostle in the Gospel. So much for the idea that because women are not ordained as officers in the Church, they have no role to play. When you are called a fellow worker in the Gospel by such a man as Paul, that does not imply your role is only knitting socks for the elderly (which, as an elderly, I applaud), but that you are active in winning the lost and training young believers to know and grow. It is strongly implied they worked harmoniously together and with Paul in the growing of the Church. They both were highly valued and deeply appreciated by the Apostle. Both had their names in the Book of Life. They were true believers. BUT there seems to have arisen a misunderstanding between them which threatened the unity and thus the witness of the Church. So serious was this that the Apostle risked their anger and embarrassment by publicly calling on them to amend their ways and return to their once productive relationship in the Lord. This in turn would imply an appeal to pray together, respect and love each other, and work with each other in spite of any differences they might have.

Understanding how difficult this might be, Paul then enlists a mature believer, who also worked in harmony with him and these two strong-willed women, to come alongside and assist them in this reconciliation.

What a noble undertaking, what a needed ministry in the Body of Christ. I do not know just who will be accorded the highest place and role in heaven, but I strongly suspect it will be the people who hear this call and step forward to effect loving reconciliation among feuding believers, and thus restore peace to the body that the work of the Kingdom be not hindered or diminished. Whatever role this beloved brother may have had in the past at Philippi, his most important role is now before him, and maybe yours is the same. Is not this call something of what is involved in "discerning the body" as a requirement for communion? When Jesus said, "Blessed are the peacemakers, for they shall be called the children of God," He probably had in mind such a situation.

But is this how we usually handle dissension and misunderstanding in the Church? No, probably not. Rather, we usually divide up in camps, with each offended party doing their best to get more people "on their side" than the other party, thinking this proves one or the other is right, which never solves anything, but enlarges and increases the problems.

So, Paul appeals to a leading man of influence to come alongside these women and help them overcome their difficulties. We aren't sure who this "yokefellow" was, but the Greek word 'Syzygus' may also be a personal name and, if so, the appeal may be even more effective. Whoever he was, God had put him in a position to bring peace to the congregation, and restore fellowship between once valuable workers that they could again be seen as fellow workers in the Gospel. The two ladies involved will also know that Syzygus had the confidence of Paul to handle this most difficult situation, so they were more likely to give heed to his advice. The point being that if these two women are once more occupied in the work of the Kingdom instead of being pre-occupied with their differences, the unity of the Body will be restored along with their usefulness and the added assurance their names are in the Book of Life. For whoever helps believers to become reconciled covers a multitude of sin, and promotes health in the Body of Christ.

Questions for Discussion and Reflection

1. What does it mean to "stand fast in the Lord"?

2. What does it mean to "labor in the Gospel"?

3. Why is Paul so concerned that unity be restore in the Philippian church?

4. How might understanding that our citizenship is in heaven strengthen our efforts toward unity with one another?

5. What repercussions does dissension among believers have on the work of the Church, both locally and globally?

6. What repercussions does dissension among believers have on our personal efforts to stand firm in the faith?

19

REJOICE AND GIVE THANKS!
Philippians 4:4-7

You are in prison, and waiting for the decision to be handed down. Will you live or die? Will you be set free or remained chained day and night to your guards? You know that some of your dearest friends on earth are really suffering and may also face death soon. Within, you are haunted by your past sins. The prospects are dim. By all standards commonly accepted by all people, life is not good. So what will you say in what may be the last letter you will ever be allowed to write to your loved ones and friends?

I would probably write something like this: "Please pray for me. Pray that God would move the heart of the judge to set me free; he knows I'm innocent. Please pray that the food might improve and that all these sores on my ankles and wrists would be healed. Please pray that there will be no more beatings; my back is so raw and sore." In my better moments, I would probably tell my friends that, "I am praying for you, that somehow you might hold on and that God would protect you from harm and danger, and provide all your needs."

The man in prison was Paul. All the above realities were facing him. So what did he say in this part of the letter he wrote to the Philippians? "Rejoice in the Lord always, and again I say rejoice!" In fact, these words sum up this entire epistle. It is truly called the Epistle of Joy.

In these few verses from chapter four, we discover the secret to true blessedness and peace in life. Let me walk you through these words and help you experience what this man knew and experienced no matter what the outward prospects life held for him.

I. VERSE 4: REJOICE IN THE LORD ALWAYS, AND AGAIN I SAY REJOICE

Was Paul insane or in denial? Remember what his circumstances were? But this sort of rejoicing never depends on circumstances but on the Lord. If Paul was crazy, then so was Jesus, because in the upper room He talked a lot about joy and rejoicing, and He was only hours away from being betrayed, denied, and forsaken by His disciples, cruelly whipped and tortured, and finally death on the cross. And He talked about joy and rejoicing? But notice the words again. "Rejoice IN THE LORD always, and again I say rejoice."

Yes, a Christian may and should be joyful within, even when all the outward circumstances are sad and dreary. Why? Because our rejoicing is in the Lord, not in circumstances. But that sort of joy and rejoicing must be cultivated and developed. It is a part of the fruits of the Spirit. But unless we commit to it and meditate on the reasons for it, we will think but little of it. And just what are these reasons? The

Father loves you so much He gave His Son for you. Jesus loves you so much He died for you. The Spirit loves you so much He lives in you. Shall I go on? All your sins have been forgiven. You are adopted as God's child. God has a place in heaven for you, and Jesus is coming again. Again I say, rejoice.

II. VERSE 5: LET YOUR GENTLENESS BE EVIDENT TO ALL; THE LORD IS AT HAND

Do you know how many words it would take in the English language to translate that word "gentleness" from the Greek? Try these for a start: big-heartedness, forbearance, kindliness, sweetness, reasonableness, consideration, generosity, friendliness, patience. It would take these and many more to capture what the Holy Spirit is saying. So, if you want to experience blessings and peace and inner joy, you have to be willing to help others experience these things, according to their needs. Think about how full and wonderful life could be if you were this sort of person. Think how many people would go to bed every night thanking God for you and the privilege of being a part of your life. Why should you be this way? Because the Lord is at hand. That means your life is lived in His sight and presence, and also that He is coming again, and all the blessings and joys of belonging to Him will be fully experienced.

III. VERSE 6: BE ANXIOUS FOR NOTHING, BUT IN EVERYTHING BY PRAYER AND SUPPLICATION, WITH THANKSGIVING, LET YOUR REQUESTS BE MADE KNOWN UNTO GOD

Here we enter the very heart of what prayer and life is all about. "Be anxious for nothing" does not eliminate kindly interest or godly concern for others. What it means is that we should not allow fearful and fretful worry to control our lives as many people do. Most of our worries are about our own personal interests such as what we eat, wear, or the future of what may happen. The cure for worry is prayer. So, instead of being controlled by anxiety, we go to Him who has promised to answer prayer and to make all things work together for our ultimate good, salvation, and likeness to Christ.

Notice the contrast: "Be anxious for nothing, but in EVERYTHING by prayer and supplication..." I think the immediate context would suggest mainly the things which might cause us fear. Peter put it this way, "Cast all your cares on Him, because He cares for you." Many people give in to anxiety with mere apathy, but there's nothing apathetic about prayer and supplication. In fact, that suggests continuous and fervent prayer. And we are to do this with thanksgiving. This implies a humble acceptance of God's will, knowing that His will is always best. It also calls on us to gratefully remember all God's many past and present blessings, and have confidence in the future care He extends us. Prayer without thanksgiving is like a bird without wings; it doesn't get off the ground.

Then we may bring our petitions before the Lord. This means definite, specific requests. When we come before the Lord, we need to understand these two things: Nothing is too great for His power to accomplish, and nothing is too small for His love to be concerned about.

IV. VERSE 7: AND THE PEACE OF GOD WHICH PASSES ALL UNDERSTANDING WILL GUARD YOUR HEARTS AND MINDS THROUGH CHRIST JESUS

So, if joy fills our hearts, and loving concern for others is our spirit, and constant, believing, submissive, and grateful prayer is our practice, the result will always be peace. Not a peace of self-trust or favorable circumstances and consequences, but the sweet peace Jesus knew even in the garden of Gethsemane, which was a gift from the Father. It is called "sweet peace, the gift of God's love." I am always amazed at this gift and never fully understand it, but live by it. It is a wonderful gift that we are never able to fully explain or even comprehend, but which comes to us when we follow this perfect path laid out in God's Word. It is like going on a journey and knowing that if we follow directions, we will get there, but it is still amazing. And it guards our hearts and minds. We have entered an impregnable fortress which is guarded by invincible guards which no earthly power may ever overcome. Or to put it another way, we have been given a powerful antibiotic which no germ of worry will ever overcome to destroy us. But you have to follow the path God shows us to enter that fortress and you have to accept the injection to resist the deadly disease of life controlling anxiety and fear.

Questions for Discussion and Reflection

1. What is Paul's justification to rejoice in the Lord? What is yours?

2. In the context of Paul's teaching, what does it mean to be gentle?

3. What does it mean to be "anxious for nothing"?

4. According to Paul, what is the secret to true blessedness and peace in this life?

20

THE PATHWAY OF BLESSINGS, COMMANDS, AND PROMISES
Philippians 4:4-7

I. VERSE 4

"Rejoice in the Lord always, and again I say rejoice." These words are an emphatic command and also a determined choice. Simple to understand on the surface, but it certainly doesn't make much sense to most people, especially when they are going through severe trials. Keep in mind that it was written by a man who had known little but severe trials for most of his adult life, and even when he wrote this he was in prison, facing a very possible death sentence to be handed down at any moment. Knowing that, let's at least listen to what he said, and try to understand these are not just as his words, but as God's word through him.

There are two things said, both of which seem strange and unreasonable. First of all, how do you command joy? Secondly, how is it possible to rejoice always? We have so many reasons not to rejoice.

Maybe like me, you find this command to be not only difficult to obey, but the most difficult of all God's commands.   Overwhelmed by debts; distressed by loved ones' sickness, suffering, confinement to nursing homes, or deep into Alzheimer's; kids failing in school, or even worse in rebellion against you and the Lord; unpleasant working conditions; and uncertainty about the future, we are commanded to "rejoice in the Lord always, (and in case we didn't hear it the first time) again I say rejoice."

Here is a man who was still haunted by past sins, though he was confident of being forgiven, whose friends were suffering because under his ministry they became believers. He continued to see many devastating problems ongoing in the churches he established, and he was accused of being insincere by some within the churches. He had suffered untold misery because he was serving Christ, and was now in prison, his life hanging by a thread which was held in the hands of a madman named Caesar Nero. Therefore, it is obvious that the abounding joy which leaps off every page of this letter had nothing to do with the circumstances surrounding him. But his rejoicing was in the Lord, and ours must be, too, or it will be shallow and short-lived.

II. VERSE 5

"Let your gentleness be known to all men." I love Dr. Hendriksen's translation of this verse. "Let your big-heartedness be known to all men." He then goes on to say that there are many like words one may use to express this same truth. Some he lists are forbearance, kindliness, sweet reasonableness, considerateness, generosity, and others. But all these together help to convey the kind of person all believers are commanded to be. There is no one English word which really conveys the richness of this word in the original. Because we are united to Christ, we will never find joy unless we strive to be a blessing to others. This command shows us that the pathway of true blessedness cannot be walked by one who always insists on his own way and is always seeking to be recognized as the deserving leader. The mature Christian knows it is far better to suffer wrong than to inflict wrong.

When Paul said, "Let your sweet reasonableness be known to ALL," he meant just that. Certainly it begins within the body of believers of which you are a part, but it must also be obvious to all who know and observe your behavior. When we read "The Lord is at hand," we know this implies the supreme motivation for all our behavior. And this doesn't JUST mean we know the Lord is coming back some day, but that He is always at hand. We live in His presence every moment of every day. With this consciousness present, and when it is present, our behavior becomes more than a private matter. But this does also have the meaning that since we believe the Lord is coming back, and since we must all appear before His judgment seat, and since He said, "Beloved, avenge not yourselves, but rather give place to wrath, for vengeance is mine, I will repay saith the Lord," we can well afford to be big-hearted and gentle with others, even those who drive us up a wall sometimes. Our time here on earth is very, very brief at best. So, whether we think of the Lord's physical and final return from heaven, or whether we understand that soon, very soon for all of us, we will appear before Him, our "big-heartedness," our forbearance of each other, our gentleness with each other should appear to all people.

III. VERSE 6a

"Be anxious for NOTHING." This reads more accurately, "Stop being so fretful and overly anxious." Now, there is such a thing as kindly concern for others and in the right sense, even for one's self. When Paul in another place mentioned his catalog of suffering, he listed his daily concern for the churches. But in this context, he is speaking about being unduly concerned or worried about things you simply have to trust God for, like the things we spend most of our time worried sick (literally) over. This might be what we shall eat, what we shall wear, how we look and how we can improve it, how long we're going to live, and all the multitudes of cares we allow to dominate our lives. Well, the cure for this sort of anxiety is believing, trusting prayer which is filled with praise. It is not relapsing into apathetic indifference, nor is the answer to anxiety inactivity. We look at the next part of this verse to find the cure.

IV. VERSE 6b

"But in everything, by prayer and supplication, with thanksgiving, let your requests be made known to God." Even as we are told to be anxious in nothing, now we are told, "But in EVERYTHING, by prayer and supplication, with thanksgiving, let you petitions be made known to God." In all situations in which you are tempted to waste away with worry and care, take it to the Lord in prayer. As Simon Peter put it, "Cast all your cares on Him, because He cares for you."

There are four words here which are related and often used interchangeably, but not when they are used consecutively. The first of these is PRAYER. This is a comprehensive word which means coming before God in any form of address, whether confession, rejoicing, seeking, etc. Under the general heading of prayer, Paul uses the word SUPPLICATION. This is a word that recognizes our unworthiness and renounces any claim to equality with the one to whom we come with our requests. It speaks of humility, and yet of urgent need. The next word is THANKSGIVING. This acknowledges the sovereignty of God and faithful trust in His answer to any request. In 1 John 5:14-15, we are assured, "Now this is the confidence we have in Him, that if we ask anything according to His will, He hears us. And if we know that He hears us, we know we have the petitions we ask of Him." Thanksgiving includes and really begins with giving God praise for Himself and His saving grace. It means we remember past blessings and the many answers to prayer in the past. It means awareness of present blessings and confidence for the future answers. I think of Jesus at the tomb of Lazarus before commanding Lazarus to "come forth." He first prayed, "Father, I thank You that You have heard Me and that You always hear Me ..." That should be the spirit of thanksgiving which precedes specific requests. Someone once said, "Prayer without thanksgiving is like a bird without wings."

The last of these four words is REQUESTS, but more properly translated, PETITIONS. This word implies very specific and even well thought out requests of God. It is far more than just "Bless me and mine," or even "Bless all the missionaries on home and foreign fields." Praying in vague generalities to God makes no more sense than going to your earthly father when you have a specific need and just saying, "Daddy, please give me what I need or want." When Jesus taught us to pray in what we call "The Lord's Prayer," the petitions are orderly and specific, and to begin with He had said, "After this manner therefore pray." Just remember Paul said, "Let your petitions be made known UNTO GOD." Praying is not "wishing upon a star," nor is it addressed, "To Whom it May Concern," but unto GOD, who is all powerful, all merciful, and whom Jesus granted us the right to call "our Father." And we read in Psalm 103, "Like as a father pities his children, so the Lord pities those who fear Him. For He knows our frame, He remembers that we are but dust."

V. VERSE 7

The blessed results. It all ties together. If we are rejoicing in the Lord always, and if our magnanimous spirit is evident to all, and if we lay aside our anxiety and fretfulness, if in everything by prayer and supplication with thanksgiving make our petitions known unto God, THEN, "The peace of God which passes all understanding will guard our hearts and minds through Christ Jesus." This is the peace which Jesus talked about in the upper room when He said, "Peace I leave with you, My peace I give unto you, not as the world gives, give I to you ... These things I have spoken to you that in Me you may have peace. In the world, you will have tribulation, but be of good cheer, I have overcome the world." This peace comes from God and flows out of our relationship with Him. It is rooted in grace, and it is the "sweet peace, the gift of God's love" of which we sing. It is mentioned in every one of Paul's epistles, and always associated with grace. As someone has said, "It is the heart's calm in Calvary's storm."

It passes all human understanding. Because from a human point of view, peace only comes with favorable circumstances, Christ's gift of peace is never rooted in being at peace with the world and enjoying worldly pleasures. In fact, more often than not, the kind of peace Paul is talking about comes in the midst of turmoil, strife, and opposition from the world.

This peace stands guard over our hearts and minds especially when we are assaulted by Satan and the world, and even when we feel overwhelmed by our own failures. It keeps our minds safe, even when we are troubled by the multitudes that fall for the Gnostic nonsense as represented by such things as books or movies which totally pervert the truth of God's Word, and even distorts the facts of history, replacing sober truth with unbelieving fantasies.

Do you want to find the pathway of blessing? It is clearly marked out for us in this Scripture. Walk this well-marked path and blessing awaits you as you walk it, even before you reach the end.

Questions for Discussion and Reflection

1. Discuss the need to rejoice in the Lord always.

2. Because we are united to Christ, our joy is contingent upon being a blessing to others. Why is this? How are we called to be a blessing to others? How are you a blessing to others?

3. In this portion of the epistle, what does Paul state is the ultimate motivation for all of our behavior?

4. How do you respond to the instruction, "Be anxious for nothing"? How do you manage stress and anxiety in your life?

5. How might you apply Paul's exhortation to let go of anxiety "in everything by prayer and supplication with thanksgiving let your requests be made known to God" to your life?

6. Discuss the distinctions between prayer, supplication, thanksgiving, and requests/petitions as presented in this chapter.

21

LEARNING CONTENTMENT

Philippians 4:10-21

The Discontentment Virus has infected the vast percentage of Americans, and probably most other nationalities as well. Yes, even Christians. It has created a restlessness and a vague but powerful unhappiness which is hard to explain, given we are the wealthiest people ever to inhabit the world and have more conveniences and "toys" than the richest kings of the past. Yet, we are also the most dissatisfied of all peoples of all generations. The more we get, the more we want, and we see this reflected in every area of our society and at every level. The never-ending drive to get more, enjoy more, moving ever upward in buying power and in status is all-consuming, with few exceptions.

The one area in which I am most knowledgeable is the ministry. A part of my work at seminary was involved with placing young graduates into ministry positions, and also assisting current minister to find other calls. There was a constant flow of letters and phone calls from ministers seeking to move to another field. A few years ago, the Stated Clerk of our General Assembly reported that well over half of the ministers in the denomination wanted to move to another church (larger, of course). The average tenure of ministers overall is less than three years, and the average tenure of assistant pastors and youth ministers is under one year. The same thing is true of congregations wishing and praying their pastors will be led elsewhere. As for membership in local churches, that, too, is in a state of constant flux. In fact, the rate of turnover is such that many congregations no longer have official membership status, but people just come and go as they will. Pastors are pressured both from within local congregations and from peers to try almost anything in programs and worship to attract people and build up the size of their congregations. There are, of course, many happy exceptions to these symptoms of unrest and discontent.

What, then, could a passage like this one from Philippians, written by a man in prison and awaiting a probable death sentence, possibly say to our restless discontent generation about contentment? If this was indeed the source instead of the channel, we might well wonder. But since we believe the Bible is God's inspired word, and that it is not only true but timeless, then we believe God had chosen Paul, his circumstances, and his experiences to teach us a much needed lesson about how to learn contentment and thus to be both shining lights and towers of unmovable strength in this restless and discontented world in which we live.

I. VERSE 10: GRATITUDE AND JOY AS THE FOUNDATION OF CONTENTMENT

The Apostle begins this section by expressing deep and joyful appreciation for his fellow believers in Philippi and the way they had rallied to his side. His rejoicing was "in the Lord" because he knew what was happening through these fellow believers was a sign that Christ was working and living in them. That meant his labor of love had not been in vain, and he found great contentment and joy in seeing their growth in grace as expressed in their loving care of him. He knew they had been concerned for him all along, but lacked opportunity to show it when he first arrived in Rome as a prisoner. But as soon as possible, and as they became aware of his circumstances and condition, they began to make plans to supply his needs and extend assurances of their great love for him.

When Paul said he "rejoiced greatly in the Lord," it was not primarily over whatever gifts of food, clothing, or other needs he might have received, but over the evidence of true compassionate love for him and their willingness to sacrificially meet those needs. Let me suggest that there is much, even in these words, which points towards the secret of learning contentment. His joy was in the Lord and in the fellowship he found in their concern for him. When our eyes are opened to the many spiritual blessings God supplies for us, and not the least of which is the sharing of loving concern for each other, we are less concerned about material things, no matter how badly we may need them, or think we do. Which is better, a gift or the love of the giver? So, Paul quickly moves to make sure they understand he is not hinting for more gifts, but just rejoicing in the evidences of their spiritual health and growth.

II. VERSES 11 & 12: THE PROCESS OF DEVELOPING A SPIRIT OF CONTENTMENT

He does this by assuring the Philippians that he is not speaking out of a sense of need, for he has learned over the passing of years and many experiences the great blessing of being content in whatever circumstances and providence his commitment to Christ might lead him. I'm sure the road had not been easy, for his circumstances had changed radically since his conversion to Christ. I am so glad he used the expression, "I have learned," which indicates a process of self-discipline and growing in grace. It had not happened all at once. Though his conversion was dramatically sudden, his developing the graces which accompany salvation was a process, just as it is for us.

There was a time when he was obviously not content with his physical infirmities and pain, for he had gone before the Lord with a fervent request, often repeated, that he might be delivered of "a thorn in the flesh." It was not until he was assured that his condition was in line with God's will for his life, and that God's grace would be sufficient for him to live with the "thorn," that he was content to have it so. I don't know over what period of time this had gone on, but the indication is that it had been for some time, perhaps even a long period before he found the contentment and peace to enable him to live with his infirmity.

So, the Apostle begins to recount his varied experiences and circumstances, and once more uses the expression, "I have learned" to describe how he was able to deal with these tests and changes. Let's look more closely at what he says in verse 12. He said, "I know how to be abased." What did he mean by that? Not once, but as a continual experience, the Apostle had been brought into dire circumstances. Just a glance at the book of Acts, and even more as the Apostle shared his experiences in his epistles, we discover a man who had lived on the edge of poverty and death most of his Christian life. He had experienced hunger and thirst, coldness and nakedness, physical and mental suffering, pain, persecution, ship wreck, personal assaults from robbers, and a host of other privations. He had suffered from lack of comforts we take for granted, and he lived each day not knowing if he would survive for another, even to the point of resigning himself to what seemed to be inevitable death. But none of these things had robbed him of peace and contentment. Indeed, this was a part of learning to be content.

How about those times of abundance? Yes, there had been such times, though rarely after he became a Christian. As a Pharisee – and most likely a member of the Sanhedrin, at least in some capacity – Saul would have enjoyed a measure of wealth and most certainly power. There is also some indication that he did enjoy seasons of relative abundance along the way as a believer and missionary. Not, of course, what we would think of as abundance, but as compared to his lean times certainly an improvement. Perhaps during his pre-Christian days, he would not have been content with such limited provision either. But now as a dedicated servant of the Lord Jesus, along with food, shelter, and fellowship, he also had the excitement of seeing his efforts bearing much fruit, which gave to him great joy, peace of mind, and, of course, contentment with his lot. So, according to his standards and values, he was almost rolling in wealth.

Not all ministers and missionaries would share this definition of abundance. One of the most dangerous things which all Christian workers face is the temptation to believe in the words of a certain televangelist, "We are serving the King, why shouldn't we live as princes?" When we do not know how to honor Christ when we "abound," or even recognize that we are indeed "abounding," then we are in grave danger of becoming servants of Mammon and being held in bondage to things and the people who supply our wants and encourage our worldly ambitions. It may be a sign of greater spiritual maturity for a believer to say, "In my abundance, I am content," than to say the same in times of want.

I. VERSE 13: THE BLESSED RESULTS OF CONTENTMENT

"I can do all things through Christ who strengthens me." These words often quoted are seldom quoted in context. But what well-known verses of Scripture ARE usually quoted in their proper context? This implies a close bonding with the Lord Jesus. This implies a daily walk with Him. This implies a Christ-like sense of priorities. (The Son of Man came not to be ministered to, but to minister and to give His life up as a ransom for many.) When Christ is the fountainhead for your life, your joy, your love and energy, then He will truly enable you to not only endure, but to rejoice in Him, even in times of distress, sorrow, disappointment with life, illness, and grief. Then your testimony will be blended with that of the Apostle, and your life will bear witness to that godly Christ-like and Christ-inspired contentment. Then you may sing from your heart, "Jesus, Thou joy of loving hearts, thou fount of life, thou light of men, from the best bliss that earth imparts, we turn unfilled to Thee again. We taste Thee, O thou living bread, and long to feast upon Thee still. We drink of Thee the fountainhead, and thirst our souls from Thee to fill."

Questions for Discussion and Reflection

1. What did Paul see in the Philippian church that brought him joy?

2. What is the significance of the way in which the Philippians cared for Paul in his need?

3. What was the key to Paul's contentment? How did he learn to be content?

4. Are you content? If so, what provides your contentment? If not, what can you draw from Paul's experience to begin to work toward genuine contentment?

5. In what kind of things did Paul find abundance? Where are similar sources of abundance in your life?

6. Reflect upon verse 13 in context of the epistle. What does Paul really mean by, "I can do all things through Christ who strengthens me"?

www.ingramcontent.com/pod-product-compliance
Lightning Source LLC
Chambersburg PA
CBHW070442090426
42735CB00012B/2445